THE
CASTLETON
MASSACRE

THE CASTLETON MASSACRE

Survivors' Stories of the Killins Femicide

SHARON ANNE COOK
MARGARET CARSON

DUNDURN
PRESS

Publisher and acquiring editor: Scott Fraser | Editor: Juliet Sutcliffe
Cover and interior designer: Karen Alexiou
Cover image: torn paper: rawpixel.com
All images courtesy of the authors and Brian Killins, except "Colborne, 1960," on page 140, courtesy of Jane Moore.

Library and Archives Canada Cataloguing in Publication

Title: The Castleton massacre : survivors' stories of the Killins femicide / Sharon Anne Cook, Margaret Carson.
Names: Cook, Sharon A. (Sharon Anne), 1947- author. | Carson, Margaret (Margaret Louise), author.
Identifiers: Canadiana (print) 20220201838 | Canadiana (ebook) 20220202494 | ISBN 9781459749863 (softcover) | ISBN 9781459749870 (PDF) | ISBN 9781459749887 (EPUB)
Subjects: LCSH: Killins, Robert. | LCSH: Murder—Ontario—Castleton.
Classification: LCC HV6535.C33 C37 2022 | DDC 364.152/30971357—dc23

We acknowledge the support of the Canada Council for the Arts and the Ontario Arts Council for our publishing program. We also acknowledge the financial support of the Government of Ontario, through the Ontario Book Publishing Tax Credit and Ontario Creates, and the Government of Canada.

Dundurn Press
1382 Queen Street East
Toronto, Ontario, Canada M4L 1C9
dundurn.com, @dundurnpress 𝕏 f ⌾

Dedicated to those who were silenced in 1963

Florence Irene with her unborn baby
Mother, partner, sister, aunt, gardener, harmonica player

Pearl Irene with her full-term unborn baby
Daughter, wife, sister, friend, musician, mother-to-be

Patricia Elizabeth Anne
*Daughter, sister, friend, forever waiting for the tooth fairy
to come for her two front teeth*

Ada Gladys with her beloved dog, Taffy
Sister, aunt, sister-in-law, mediator, talented artist

CONTENTS

———

PROLOGUE

On the morning of Friday, May 3, 1963, I emerged from my bedroom in my pyjamas to have breakfast with my parents at our home in Calgary, Alberta. At sixteen, I was a typical high school student in perpetual motion. Breakfast and dinner were family times, with my animal-nutritionist father carefully charting my daily intake of protein.

I stopped partway into the kitchen at the sight before me: my parents were both sitting, ashen-faced, staring at each other as the CBC Radio national news reported on happenings in Canada and around the world.[1] The radio sat on the end of the Arborite counter, close to the breakfast nook with a standard Formica-topped table and matching padded chairs in turquoise and chrome. Neither of my parents moved to turn off the radio, as they often did when wanting to encourage conversation with their teenage daughter.

Both continued to sit in silence and glance distractedly at me. "What's going on?" I asked. Abruptly, my mother got up from her chair and dished out my breakfast, just as she always did. A tall and elegant woman, she was dressed as neatly as ever; her hair had been carefully combed and she was ready as usual to tackle the day before her. Undeterred by their lack of response, I chattered away, finished my breakfast, and headed back to my bedroom to get changed for school.

As I was about to go out the door, my mother stopped me. Composing herself, she delivered a carefully worded speech; it ran something like this: "When you get home from school, neither of us will be here. We are going on a trip, and we don't know how long we will be away. A woman will arrive in an hour or so to care for your grandmother and prepare your meals. There will be a letter for you from us on the dining-room table. Please read it carefully and do as we ask." Her formality of speech and rigid stance remain clear in my mind today.

I agreed, albeit a bit perplexed. I bade them goodbye, assured my grandma that I would be home right after school, grabbed my lunch and my homework, and rushed out of the house. As I walked, I reflected about how odd it was that Mom hadn't told me where they were going on this impromptu trip, and that she didn't know how long they would be away. My parents were not impulsive people, so I trusted that they would organize everything.

After school, there was indeed a letter waiting for me, and as I read it, I sank onto the sectional couch in disbelief.

> Dad and I are flying to Ontario today to be with your cousins, Peggy and Brian. We anticipate being back in about ten days, but we will call you long-distance when we know more. A terrible thing has happened. Your Uncle Bob has murdered his family, Florence, Gladys, Pearl, and little Patsy. I feel very emotional as I write this because we have been in touch recently with Florence and I know she feared for her life. She was pregnant, and the baby was also killed. Pearl was close to delivering her baby, so that makes six people Bob has killed. I know that this will be a shock to you and I am sorry not to be there to cushion this, but we did not want you to hear about this first on tonight's national news.
>
> We might be returning with Peggy, and if so, I will need a lot of help from you.
> Love, Mom

A collage of newspaper headings from 1963.

I let the contents of the letter wash over me. My memory went back to the breakfast scene I had unwittingly interrupted. I realized that when I found my parents sitting staring at each other that morning, they had just heard the newscast of a mass murder in Castleton, Ontario. The perpetrator was my father's older brother, Robert, a former United Church minister.

Fifty-six years later, Margaret — the "Peggy" my mother mentioned — and I embarked on a project to understand what happened that day and what had led up to it in the years before that set the scene for a mass murder. The journey to an understanding of the short- and long-term causes, the events on that horrifying day, and the process by which the survivors moved beyond the trauma of their lives has been intense and, occasionally, very painful. It has also been healing for the two survivors, Margaret and her younger brother, Brian. They have lived almost their whole lives with this tragedy hovering in the background. Over one short Thursday evening in May 1963, a man they had feared for years murdered their pregnant mother, little sister, pregnant older sister, and aunt. At the time of the massacre, the perpetrator was living outside their back door in a shack, charting every move the family made to and from their homes.

The mayhem of that night extended beyond the killings, however. Brian watched as a family friend engaged in hand-to-hand combat with the assailant to try to protect him and his sisters during the murderous frenzy; Brian was blown into a corner by a shotgun with his hair singed from the blast; he watched in shock as his teacher was shot repeatedly by the murderer. Margaret also witnessed the bloody combat and survived by hiding under a bed, finding herself staring directly into the murderer's eyes as she cowered in the dark against the bedframe that held her captive; both children ran for their lives and survived, but at a huge cost.

Memory, trauma, grief, regret, and healing all figure in the aftermath of this horrific event. The role of the perpetrator, while seemingly straightforward as a malicious madman, was also multi-faceted. One might imagine that he can only be understood as heartless and evil, and yet in addition to being a vicious gunman he was also a brother and a son, and a much-admired brother and son at that. My own father, a kind and intelligent man, was also the perpetrator's younger sibling. Unable to process what his beloved brother had done, he thought of him only as a "good man" who made one big mistake. Incomprehensibly, he even wrote a long letter to the surviving children years after Robert had wiped out their entire family in which he all but begged them to reconsider Robert in a positive light. Robert had a kind of dark charisma that captured the sympathy and admiration of even the most decent of people: a mixture of coiled fury, a hair-trigger temper that forced everyone into making compromises, and a momentary charm that soon became manipulative. Long before the murders, many people found Robert scary.

A Family Memoir

This book is a family memoir. Families are complex structures: they have an internal history that is understood only by its members, and often understood differently by each individual member. They are the fundamental institutions that allow children to make meaning of the world they encounter. There are happy times in any family, and there are pressure points that emerge in response to family members' personalities and larger events. Sometimes families fracture, but not completely, with some family members retaining loyalties and bonds with past family members. Other family members can feel caught in a liminal zone, partly in one family, partly in another. And any family has an organizational structure, with some individuals — usually parents — wielding more authority than others. We aim to show that the family at the heart of this story demonstrates all of these characteristics.

The story of how a clergyman became a mass murderer explores one fractured family where several members had difficulty in cutting the bonds that had held them together in better times. The ambivalent position of the estranged father, Robert, especially with his daughter, led to confusion, stalking, and eventually femicide. In trying to understand how the murderer saw his rights and responsibilities within the various family groupings, we have attempted to reconstruct the perspectives of all of the members of the family as they responded to his frenetic efforts to maintain his position of authority. As a family memoir, this reconstruction has given us some insight into the baffling decisions made by this murderer, and perhaps illuminates some of the dark corners of other instances of domestic violence that lead to murder.

There is more than one family considered here. In fact, there are eight permutations of three families in this account, with only the two surviving children finding themselves in the last four.

First, there was the Killins family, into which Robert was born. Like so many families at the turn of the twentieth century, Robert's parents, Robert John and Rachel, were poor farmers. To make their fortune, they took up homestead lands in Alberta. Robert John nominally headed this family, but in practice Rachel set the family values and sought betterment for her children through education. The eldest daughter, Gladys, eventually became a noted watercolourist. Robert was the second child and the family's undisputed "star." My father, Harold, was the youngest in the family.

The second family profiled are the Frasers, whose daughter Florence married thirty-one-year-old Robert in 1938 when she was eighteen years of age. The Fraser Family was working-class and also had a dominant mother who determined the family's values. Pearl Viola and Ira Fraser's marriage was far more fractious than the Killinses', causing Florence to create an escape plan into an early marriage.

Robert and Florence wed in 1938, and their daughter, Pearl, was born in 1944. This family is at the crux of this family memoir. The family broke down but was never formally dissolved as Robert refused a divorce. On Robert and Florence's separation, Pearl found herself still in close proximity to Robert, trailed and tracked by him as he stalked her every move. Furthermore, she was often drawn back to him through her loyalty to him as her father. This ambivalent relationship with Robert must have been deeply confusing for her, and for Robert, too. On the fracturing of the family unit, both Robert and Pearl were thrown into a liminal zone, no longer in the original family unit, but also not in the new unit either. Robert was cast completely outside; Pearl was somewhere between the two.

Florence then created another family with A.D. (Austin Davis) Hall, having three children with him: Margaret, Brian, and Patsy. With Pearl, that family survived for about sixteen years until A.D.'s death in 1962. Robert remained close at hand, living in a series of one-room shacks he built for himself immediately outside the family residence, and stalking their every move. In exerting his authority over Pearl, and to a lesser extent his estranged wife, Florence, Robert became a kind of outlier member of Florence and A.D.'s family. He watched and waited from this vantage point, a dark presence.

After A.D.'s death, a new family was just getting started with Florence and her new partner, Tom Major, in 1963. They had announced their departure for northern Ontario with Margaret, Brian, and Patsy. Pearl had married and was about to give birth to her first child. Hence, neither of these two families had a chance to coalesce because Robert murdered Florence, Patsy, and Pearl before they could flee.

After the familicide, Margaret and Brian joined our family in Calgary. This family constituted my parents, Harold and Ethel, my elderly grandmother, Jessie, the two orphaned children, and myself.

Within eighteen months, this family also morphed into a new version with the addition of my brother David, who had moved back into the family home, the death of my grandmother, and my departure for university. After David's marriage, the children assumed a central role with my parents, becoming a true second family to them.

This book is a memoir of all of these families, with the unit headed by Florence and Tom little more than a promise. In the case of Robert's birth family, his own failed family, and the two families created by Florence after the destruction of her marriage to Robert, family units were critically important in shaping Robert's frustrations as well as his actions. In addition, the families shaped everyone within their boundaries, including the children.

This is also the story of a complicated courier of death and what led him to plan the murder of his family. But while he is important in making sense of the tragedy, it is not only about him. The women he killed — his estranged wife, Florence, his alienated daughter, Pearl, a six-year-old child, Patsy, and his sister, Gladys — are all central to comprehending how such a mass murder could happen. This book is as much about giving them a voice as it is about understanding a murderous misfit.

Comprehending how an award-winning scholar from Queen's University who became a United Church minister turned into a mass murderer takes us much further back than May of 1963. The roots run right back to the early twentieth century to the family that raised Robert.

Was Robert Killins mentally ill, a victim himself of some neurological disorder? We believe that he was perfectly sane from childhood through to his death and that he had planned his massacre as carefully as military commanders would plan an attack on an enemy outpost. In Robert's estimation, that is exactly what his extended family had become: enemy territory. He was what we would now call a "grievance collector": he believed he had been wronged by every family member and in many ways. In his mind, this night's deeds would right those wrongs. How does a normal, bright, and much-admired child turn into a grievance collector? We hope to answer this question.

This is also about the search to uncover the facts of the case as undertaken by two women unrelated by blood but who became sisters through circumstance. For many years, Margaret and I have debated the causes of this tragedy. Together, we worked our way through the documentary record — which is remarkably thin, considering the havoc wreaked by Robert's murders — we interviewed scores of people and pieced together the story of how and why this femicide occurred. Most crucial in reconstructing the murders, and the issues that gave rise to them, has been oral history.

Oral histories are a form of research where the interviewer and the respondent work together to tell the respondent's story. It can take the form of a crafted account in which the interviewer has little involvement, or it might be the product of questions to which the respondent replies. The version of oral history found here is a combination of my prompts and both of the survivors' memories, as well as those of our many interviewees, of the years leading up to the murders, of the events on that day and evening, and of the painful days and years afterward as they fought their fears and sought normality. Sometimes I asked questions of them, and at other times I wrote accounts to which they responded.[2] Margaret and I have been discussing the events of that night, along with the many anomalies in Robert's actions, for almost sixty years now. Our personal project must stand as one of the longest oral history exercises on record.

We have interviewed, and heard the stories of, most people associated with the events that night who are still alive, both in Castleton and beyond. We have even benefitted from the family lore handed down to the child who was born the day of the murders to a mother who sheltered the children in her home. Where participants have died, we have heard oral testimony from their children. Without these oral histories, we would not have been able to complete the research of this dire event or the characters who figure in it.

Always, we have compared and critically read the oral histories against what we thought was true from other accounts and records. In some cases, the memories offered to us were mistaken. We understand how this could occur many years on, given the nature of memory. But always we were able to take some element from each oral history and weave it into the story. We are profoundly grateful to everyone who participated in this extended exercise in oral history, even when doing so summoned unwelcome memories. The names of those who agreed to be identified are found in the acknowledgements.

Unique to this story is the fact that two of the central characters, Margaret and Brian, are still very much alive and have been deeply involved in the research and writing of this book. In terms of the Calgary period of our lives, my parents' and oldest brother's voices have been lost, to our deep regret. There have been spirited discussions and debates about the facts of that first post-murder period among the remaining family members. Not all details of each person's memories are in agreement, but through a careful process of repeated discussions on problematic details, consultation with the slender written record, literally walking through the events, and logical deduction, we have arrived at what we believe to be the facts of the case. In the end, it is the meaning each participant made of those facts that counts the most, of course. Yet there has been no dispute about Margaret's and Brian's memories and feelings in that crucial and painful phase of their recovery. They have reconstructed and told that part of their story better than any narrator could have done.

For Brian especially, the project has been searing. After the first weeks when Brian joined our family, he and I occasionally spoke of the tragedy. Since then, we had never spoken of it again until we began this project. The silence around this was also true for both children in their interactions with my parents and brothers. Surfacing the memories of those days and weeks has required more fortitude than I would have been able to summon. And yet, both survivors have persevered and unstintingly helped to reassemble this story through agonizing memories that have returned to them from years ago.

As we have tackled these difficult subjects, time after time returning to the horror and shock of those early days after their family was murdered, we have all reflected on the curious nature of memory as one digs through the layers of time. Despite my limited role in integrating the children into our family, even I have been astonished at some long-forgotten event or detail that had little meaning then yet has far more meaning now that the context is much clearer. But the shocks of suddenly recovering a memory were much greater for Margaret and Brian. At times, this involved remembering something they might have consciously suppressed in order to get through the hard times. At other times, this occurred in the middle of the night or while Margaret and I were talking through one more detail that made little sense. "Oh my goodness," Margaret would say, "I have just realized why that happened! And here is another memory to go with it!" This occurred so often in our research, often over food and in comfortable surroundings, that during our conversations I would sit with pen in hand, waiting for the breakthrough of another memory to hit Margaret so I could get it down quickly and ask for more details from her.

We have also explored the means by which the survivors managed to heal from this trauma, and the lessons we must all learn if children are to be helped in recovering from trauma. In the course of our research, we found heroes and cowards, examples of self-promotion in the face of terror, and of great kindness where self-interest was jettisoned to protect the vulnerable. We uncovered the dynamics of an extended family and community that managed to keep the peace in the face of the perpetrator's mounting agitation and anger. In the end, the conciliators could not stop the carnage, and three women and one child from one extended family were massacred.

Chapter 1

The Great Migration West: The Backstory of Robert's Family, 1900–1920

When people first met Robert Killins when he was in his fifties, they report that they found a "difficult" man with poor personal hygiene who was distrustful of others, racially and class-prejudiced, and inclined to argue loudly and impatiently. He had become a "control freak" and a stalker of his wife and daughter. He attacked his estranged wife verbally and physically and beat his daughter to the brink of death. He was isolated, sick, and at times irrational. People in his community were wary of him, with the children calling him "Iron Head" after the Frankenstein character because of his stiff gait. How had Robert developed into such a maladjusted and even malevolent adult? What kind of family helped to create him? Was he always a troubled child, or did he experience a relatively happy childhood?

The Homestead Years

When Robert's father, Robert John Killins, was born in 1869 into a

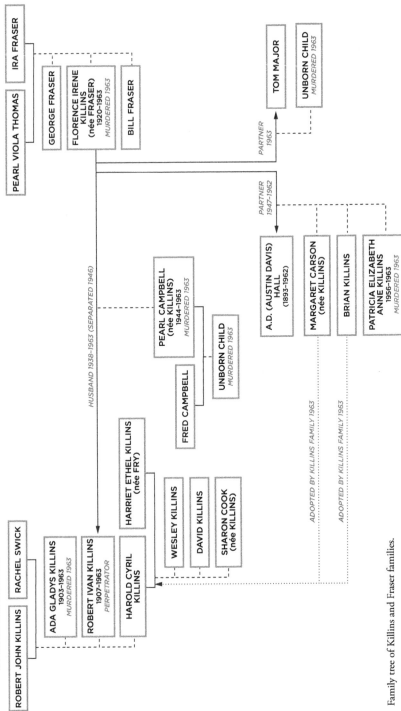

Family tree of Killins and Fraser families.

poor Ontario farming family, the Canadian West was just beginning to be opened up to white settler immigration. Manitoba would become Canada's fifth province the following year. The first Riel Rebellion in 1869 had reminded the Canadian government that the land they were about to acquire from the Hudson's Bay Company already had an established population of Indigenous and Métis people, with some white settlers around the margins. There was as yet no recognition that those lands were unceded to settler society from Indigenous Peoples.

As a child, it is not likely that Robert John would have known much about the Canadian West other than possibly to have read romantic stories of Western adventure as a teenager, standard fare for many boys in this era. He might, for example, have read some of Colonel Prentiss Ingraham's series featuring Buffalo Bill, such as *Buffalo Bill's Boy Bugler; Or, the Last of the Indian Ring*. Like so many other dime-store Western novels of the era, it featured tough and resilient male characters who were either cowboys or ranchers. Modelled on the classic frontiersmen in the American West, these men (and there were rarely women in the stories, despite a number of female authors) held to their principles, even when these were unpopular and even life-endangering; they were attractive because of their masculine vitality and certainty of their place in the universe.

Robert John's father, John Edward, had died carelessly. Family lore had it that Robert John's father had been staggering home, drunk late one night, after wasting the family's slim resources, when he stumbled while on a bridge, fell into the water, and drowned. The moral of this tale, repeated to every child in the family, was not the obvious temperance lesson, but rather that one must learn to swim.

This calamity meant that Robert John was fatherless by the age of eight. As for his widowed mother, Annie Buchanan, life became much more precarious with her husband's death. She managed to feed the family of three boys and two girls, ranging in age from three to twelve, but none of the children received much direction or education, consigning them to the ranks of casual labourers. Annie herself died in 1890, so Robert John lost his own mother when he was twenty-one.

Probably through family labour, Robert John did learn some animal husbandry and cropping on the Ontario farm where the family continued to live. In addition, he acquired basic carpentry skills that most farmers needed and possessed. It is likely that he worked as a labourer for another farmer, as his male siblings also did. Robert, then, was used to back-breaking labour before he set off to work long days and months on his own homestead.

On January 1, 1901, Robert John Killins married Rachel Swick before a Methodist preacher, one S.W. Fallis. Both of the newlyweds were older than was common for newlyweds of the era: Rachel was twenty-nine and Robert John, thirty-one. When Robert John and Rachel registered the marriage on January 10, they brought with them two witnesses, Edgar Swick, Rachel's brother, and Nellie De Potty, a family friend. The marriage and registration occurred in Caistor Township, a rural region of Lincoln County.

Rachel was two years Robert John's junior, but far beyond him in terms of education and determination. She had attended the Normal school course one summer, where she would have learned how to plan a lesson in such subjects as scientific temperance instruction or British history or Canadian geography; she would have perfected her writing script and have been shown strategies for grouping children in one-room schools. Because the older children in her school would have been expected to teach the younger ones, she also would have used peer instruction where the children would memorize passages and relate them to others. She would also have practiced elocution skills to teach the children how to "declaim" or speak eloquently.

Normal schools welcomed women in this period but usually separated them from the men for most of the curriculum. Rachel would have lived in supervised housing to preserve her virtue. The "Normal" (where novice teachers learned the "norms" of an educated society) operated like a type of finishing school for young women and men, and would have encouraged alumni to set their sights higher for their children when they started their own families.

Rachel taught elementary school for about a decade with a temporary certificate before her marriage. She would have been eligible for Normal

Rachel Killins.

school after junior matriculation, or grade 11. This would have placed her age when she began teaching at approximately eighteen, following the pattern of most female elementary school teachers in this era. In the 1880s and 1890s when Rachel began her career, teachers in country schools were predominantly female. After all, there were very few socially acceptable professions for women in this period as domestic service declined as an option for women's employment. Had Rachel rejected the notion of teaching, she could instead have become a secretary or a nurse, but not much else.

The careers of young women teachers tended to be short since they were required to quit teaching if they married, even as late as the 1950s. Any married woman who applied for a teaching position was thought to remove a job from a man, who in turn needed to support his family. The idea that some women needed to work to help support their families reflected badly on their husbands. Thus, even if the family was almost destitute, misplaced male pride supported legislation that barred a married woman from teaching.

In teaching for at least a decade before her marriage, Rachel's career was far longer than usual. We can only assume that Rachel enjoyed her career enough to maintain it. It is likely that Rachel taught in one of the many one-room schools across the province. The census shows her as living with her family in Caistor Township in 1891, so this is likely where the school was located. Teaching instilled in Rachel a profound respect for formal education and the unwavering resolution that her children would be distinguished through education. In education and in all other matters, it appears that Rachel ran the family, determining the tone and behaviour of the household.

By 1901, Robert John had become ever more the dreamer, focusing on elaborate schemes by which he could get rich. For a period, he dreamed of owning an orchard farm in Ontario's fruit belt. Then he focused on construction in the hope that building houses for other farmers would be the route to prosperity. But always the problem was a lack of capital. He needed a major fundraising project to kick-start his plans. Meanwhile, Rachel concentrated on her new baby and the many needs of her family.

The first of their children arrived on December 16, 1901, a little girl whom they named Ada Gladys. Gladys seemed to absorb her mother's nature, taking charge of matters even as a little girl. Although she was always small in stature, she had a booming voice, especially for a child. She quickly learned that she could have her way if she spoke loudly and assertively enough. Gladys had a reputation in the family as a serious, clever, and bossy little girl.

In 1903, Robert John and Rachel decided to find the capital they needed by taking up a homestead in the West. Like so many of their

Robert John Killins, about 1901.

hopeful neighbours living on Ontario farms, they boarded one of the colonist cars on a train heading west with little Gladys in tow.

The passage west on the colonist car was difficult enough, considering the crowding, food and luggage strewn about, and bunks swinging down from the ceilings. For settlers with small children, as with Robert John and Rachel, the trip must have been very stressful. Nevertheless, Robert John was as optimistic as ever, certain that the homesteading experience would be a success. Rachel was far less certain, but she loyally made many of the arrangements and gritted her teeth. As Gerald Friesen recounts, "the colonist cars became little communities in themselves."[1]

The wooden slats that comprised the seating benches could be made up into berths that would, in a pinch, accommodate a family of four. A tiny kitchen was built into the end of the car, and here the passengers prepared simple meals. Supplied with basic provisions, the emigrants embarked on the long journey through northern Ontario and on to the Prairies. When the train was held up, waiting for supply trains to go through, the passengers passed the time as they could. On arriving at a stop with stores, a stream of emigrants swarmed the establishments to replenish their provisions.

Life in a colonist car was necessarily communal. Children would have played loudly with one another. One can imagine that meals were shared, since everyone had the aromas of every other family's meal; drinking water was carried aboard and shared, too; sleeping arrangements lacked privacy, and when the children were tucked in, the adults would naturally have shared some time together, making friends as they moved closer to their new lives on the Prairies.

On this long ride to their homesteads, people shared information, fears and hopes. For a young family with children, those hopes must have been very great indeed. At the same time, the information proffered by others would have been essential, since there were few other sources to follow. Where was the most fertile land? Was it served by the main railway or a branch line? Were there active Indigenous Peoples in the area and were they friendly? We don't know if Robert John learned of a good location to stake his claim from others on the train, but he could well have done so. Both Robert John and Rachel had invested their last dollars in this venture, and if it failed, the rest of their lives would be blunted by the experience. As hard as life was in the colonist car, it was about to become even harder, and certainly lonelier, for the family once they disembarked.

The Calgary that Robert John and Rachel found on leaving the train that summer in 1903 was a bustling centre of eight thousand people.[2] It had been founded in 1875 by Inspector Brisebois of the North-West Mounted Police to help control the rum trade between settlers and Indigenous people in the area by establishing a fort. The Mounties had decided on a site at the confluence of the Bow and Elbow Rivers, in sight of the foothills and open prairie. The beauty of the location was far less important than the water source and natural protection offered by the river basin for the new fort.

In the few years that Robert John and Rachel were to spend in Calgary, the city expanded at a dizzying rate. The construction trades boomed and had difficulty keeping up with building permits issued for new dwellings. Wages were high and room and board were available for a modest sum for unattached men. By 1911, Calgary was listed as the tenth largest city in Canada, beating Edmonton, with which it had already developed a rivalry.[3] By then, the city had warehouses for goods and oil, eight hotels, two hospitals, a Carnegie library, and Mount Royal College. There were sewers, a street railway, schools, electric lighting, paved roads, and parks. Rachel was cheered by the comforts she found there.

The family arranged for temporary lodgings while Robert John took a job at Calgary's Cushing Sash and Door Factory. That he did not choose to become a hired hand on one of the farms in the area might have been due to his young family needing his support, or the fact that labourers in Calgary commanded good wages at the time, better than a farmer could offer. He worked at the factory for almost two years to create a nest egg for the homesteading costs before them. Since Robert John and Rachel had little ready cash when they arrived in Calgary, they first needed to get together enough capital to sustain themselves as homesteaders until the first crop was in. And in this quest, they were not alone.

Posters pitched to Americans shut out from the closing of the American frontier were also directed at eastern Canadians lured to cash in on the offer of free land. Marketing spurred dreams of a prosperous future. Sadly, the success rate was not good for those receiving the free land and full title. With the positive stories were many tales of homesteaders whose dreams turned to nightmares.

Between 1896 and 1914, three million people arrived in the West to take up homesteads. Stephen Leacock, in a bit of classic overstatement, noted how common it was for Canadians to homestead: "Going West, to a Canadian, is like going after the Holy Grail to a knight of King

Arthur. All Canadian families had, like mine, their Western Odyssey."[4]
This was patently false, and yet the larger point must be granted: that
the offer of a free 160 acres was a powerful incentive for many young
men, women, and families in this period. Of course, many homesteaders promptly left the Canadian West for the United States as soon as
they could. More prosperous than Canada, with a larger population and
a better-established government, many settlers continued to follow the
"Holy Grail" southward. Still, by 1914, a million people had been added
to the population in the Canadian West.

The ready market for Canadian wheat and meat meant that homesteaders often prospered once they became established. Homesteaders
with farming experience, like Robert John, were well equipped to make
the most of the opportunity they were being offered. These were "boom"
years; Robert John and Rachel had hit the market at just the right time.

Farmers taking up their hundred and sixty acres of "free" land still
had many expenses that had to be covered somehow. Anyone claiming a
quarter section, as Robert John did, agreed to build a house worth three
hundred dollars and outbuildings. He would have promised to break (or
work) thirty acres of land in total, seeding it for crops. A football field
measures about one and a third acres, as a comparison. He also promised
to live on the land for at least six months of each year for three years. This
provision was included to account for homesteaders who wanted to avoid
a long, cold, isolated winter on the land. To accomplish his duties, Robert
John needed at least a team of oxen or horses, a set of harnesses, a wagon
and a sleigh, a plough and a harrow, and preferably two of each, a seeder,
roller, mower, and rake, a reaper and binder, building materials for the
house, groceries for a year, kitchen utensils, and basic furniture.[5] The
Canadian Department of the Interior also recommended that a homesteader begin with four cows, four pigs, four sheep, and some poultry.[6]
And none of this came cheaply. It was estimated that this would cost a
family at least one thousand dollars, assuming building materials could
be found on the land, which was not always the case. In this period, a
skilled carpenter in Calgary would have made about three dollars fifty
cents a day. As an unskilled labourer, Robert John would have made no

more than twenty to thirty cents an hour or two to three dollars a day for a ten-hour day.[7] At this rate, it would have taken Robert John and Rachel about eighteen months to save the necessary funds.

To complicate and extend the process further, Robert John had a false start. The land he was given turned out to be so sandy that he thought it was non-arable. Within a year, he had abandoned his land and applied for and received another quarter section close to the original grant, near Vermillion, Alberta[8]. The homestead was much closer to Edmonton than to Calgary, but the family stayed in Calgary because the latter was the rail centre with a branch line extending to Vermillion. A spur line ran to within twelve miles of Mannville, the closest village to the homestead. The homestead was a further twelve miles from the village.

Robert John first travelled to the homestead in late October 1905, a month after Alberta officially became a province. He did not move onto the land until April 1906, when he began building his first shack. By July 1906, the family was able to join him there.

If the life of a male homesteader was hard, the lot of a homesteader's wife was often harder yet. Documents from the period describe grinding labour from sun-up to sun-down, laden with worries: "fear of imaginary Indians, fear of strangers, fear her children would wander away and get lost...."[9] Homestead wives were often isolated and lonely. Added to Rachel's burden was the fact that she had not been a typical farm wife before their move west. She had been a salaried teacher and thought of herself as having professional skills. Now she was in her mid-thirties, alone with her small daughter and pregnant with her second child, struggling to keep house, always with too few provisions and too much work.

Rachel had always worked hard, but her weekly tasks as a homesteading wife were far beyond anything she had experienced before. On Saturday, the cooking and baking would be done for any visitors who might arrive on Sunday. This involved cooking a roast of some kind, peeling potatoes, and baking bread, cakes, cookies, and pies. While there is little evidence that Rachel and Robert John socialized, she would still have prepared Sunday's meal the day before in order to avoid labour on the Sabbath. The house would also be scrubbed to provide for a day of rest with her husband on Sunday. Monday would have been another baking day, and in the evening the washing would have been placed in soaking tubs. Tuesday was washday: water was hauled from the well and heated in wash-boilers on the stove. The washing would begin as soon as the breakfast dishes were done, the cream separator scoured, the beds made, the floors swept, and the table set for dinner. To do the washing, she carried pails full of hot water from the stove to the tubs and scrubbed the laundry by hand on a washboard. The clothes were hung on a line in the summer but were draped over furniture in the house in the winter until they had dried, which might be several days. On Wednesday, she ironed and mended and baked some more. The ironing required that the "sad iron," a heavy iron block with a detachable handle, be heated first on the stove. Thursday and Friday were generally lighter days, and reserved for special projects, including more mending or canning. With no refrigeration, everything preserved for the family's meals had to be canned in crocks or glass sealers. She would have kept the coal-oil lamps filled and the wicks trimmed. She might also have had to milk the cow daily, and she would have tended the vegetable garden.[10] It is little wonder that Rachel was eager to return to a less demanding life in Ontario, where she would expect to work hard, but also to socialize with close neighbours and relatives.

Despite homesteaders being allowed to spend winters off the farm, Robert John and Rachel had nowhere else to go, making them year-round settlers. The wet springs, searing summers, rainy autumns, and frigid winters with high winds must have taken the couple back to the publicity posters they would have seen, which claimed that the Canadian West had "the best climate"! How did they get through those winters? One can scarcely imagine the loneliness, the worry for the children and the animals, the never-ending work just to survive.

The process of finding one's free grant, assessing its value and, in some cases, abandoning it and requesting another more fertile quarter section, must not have been unusual. As a knowledgeable Ontario farmer, Robert John would have been concerned at the particularly sandy soil of his first grant, and furthermore, he would have been in a position to estimate its productivity. Within a year, he had decided to concentrate on animal husbandry instead of cash crops. In 1909, when he requested deed to the land and attested to his improvement of it, he had two neighbours swear on his behalf that he had broken a total of thirty-eight acres, which is larger than Parliament Hill in Ottawa (twenty-nine acres in total). He had cropped twenty-two of those as well as making a big garden, a remarkable feat, considering he had chosen not to work a lot of the land, but instead convert it to pasture. The prairie crust could be like iron; to call it "breaking" the land was apt. Robert John owned a team of oxen, thirty-seven head of cattle, three hogs, and one horse, as well as a house valued at one hundred and fifty dollars, two stables and a granary worth one hundred and twenty-five dollars, thirty-five acres of fencing worth sixty dollars, and a well valued at twenty-five dollars, with no mortgage. In providing this summary of his hard work and investment in cattle and crops, he had more than successfully held up his end of the bargain. He received full title.

In the four and a half years he had held the homestead, Robert John attested that he had left the property for only fifteen days to buy cattle. However, that brief respite from farm life gave him fifteen more days away than his wife had. Bordering neighbours were kilometres distant and, in any case, were often single men. The loneliness and privation experienced by Rachel was so intense as to remain vivid in her mind for the remainder of her life.

With the help of a local carpenter, Robert John built a rather grand two-story log house, possibly to placate the deeply unhappy Rachel. At first, the cattle wintered in the coulee, which was a deep ravine, at the back of the house. Within the first year, Robert John built a lean-to for them on the main house, likely a "soddie," a structure with walls and often roof built of sod. In successive years, two good-sized stables were erected, one twenty feet by thirty and a second one measuring fourteen feet by twenty. We do not know the construction material, but it is likely that these, like the house, were made of logs. Robert John made this capital investment largely because of the severity of the climate, when winter temperatures could drop to minus thirty- or forty-degrees Fahrenheit and when one could expect snow anytime between September and April.

Gladys and Robert Killins, 1909.

His cattle had some grain from his lands and from Hudson's Bay lands that he rented for one cent an acre.

Robert John and Rachel's family expanded when another child, a boy, arrived in March 1907, when Gladys was five years old. Delighted with the new baby, Gladys doted on Robert Ivan, as did her parents. Despite Gladys's obvious talents, especially with art, Robert quickly became the star sibling. As the much-anticipated son, his development was watched closely and celebrated, as he developed a reputation for cleverness and fearlessness.

Harold Killins as an infant, 1910.

In June 1909, a third child, another son, arrived: Harold Cyril. Both of their sons would have been born at home with the help of a midwife. By the time of this last birth, Rachel was in her late thirties and considered an older mother by the norms of the period. Her health was uncertain, and given the onerous work required of her on a daily basis, the birth must have taxed her further. She remained in delicate health for the rest of her life, later developing diabetes and other chronic conditions.

Harold soon became part of the cheering section for Robert, remaining in awe of him throughout his life. Harold was small and sickly as a child, exhibiting no obvious talents, except a cheerful nature and un-wavering loyalty and admiration for his two older siblings.

Throughout his childhood, Harold did not impress his mother with his scholastic abilities. He was a slow reader, a poor speller, and struggled to understand principles that Robert absorbed quickly. Rachel deplored Harold's lack of confidence, surprisingly blind to her role in his halting development. Extant letters demonstrate a mother disappointed with vir-tually every marker of Harold's development, all of which had been met faster and with acclaim by Robert and before him, by Gladys. Harold's two older siblings served to contrast with his slow start in life. Nothing much was expected of Harold, while Robert Ivan's future was expected to be rosy.

Leaving the Homestead

Despite having received a full deed to the homestead, Robert John and Rachel decided to sell out and return to Ontario. Robert John was mak-ing good progress in developing his homestead and cattle herds, and he loved the Prairies and the lifestyle of ranching cattle. At the same time, he was increasingly hampered by heart problems said to have been ex-acerbated by the high altitude in Alberta. He reluctantly searched for, and found, a buyer for the homestead, the herds, and the equipment. In the bargain, he received a tidy sum, giving the family the freedom to decide their future for the first time in their lives. It is clear that Rachel did not grieve leaving Alberta, however.

By deciding to sell out, the family also followed norms of land owner-ship on the Prairies. Despite a wide range of experiences across different municipalities in the west, the percentage of homesteaders who stayed after they had received a land patent was somewhere between 25 and 30 percent. Thus, only one in three or four of the original homesteaders were still on the land by the end of a decade.[11] In having remained for more than four years on his homestead, Robert John was one of the more persistent settlers. A gregarious man by nature, he somehow with-stood the isolation. Hampered by ill health throughout his adult years, he nonetheless managed to break more soil than required, assembling a sizable herd of cattle, hogs, and a horse in addition. He did this without formal education or particular skill: he learned as he went, building a good-sized house and outbuildings. Robert John rose to the occasion, demonstrating the mettle that allowed homesteaders to succeed in this unforgiving environment.

In one respect, Robert John and his family did break with Prairie norms, however. Communities of homesteaders quickly developed social bonds that mimicked hierarchies found in urban societies. While two of Robert John's neighbours were on close enough terms to declare on his behalf before the homestead authorities, which resulted in his receiving ownership of his lands, the family seemed to make no close friends while living in the Mannville area. There is no record either of correspondence between Rachel and former neighbours once the family had moved back to Ontario. This is striking, since Rachel was literate and fond of letter-writing. It presents the family as relatively isolated in terms of social contacts, a quality that also characterized the children once they had grown to adulthood.

In the fall of 1910, Robert John and Rachel packed up their few belongings and their three children, one of whom was an infant just more than a year old, and began the long trip back to Ontario. They took the train back across the Prairies, stopping in the metropolis of Winnipeg for a few days.

Their willingness to take in Winnipeg as tourists speaks to their relative comfort in having money from the sale of the homestead. While homesteading, the family received the Eaton's catalogue with its array of clothes and goods at reasonable prices, although most of the products would have been out of reach of the Killins family. In this much-anticipated break, they visited the Winnipeg Eaton's store and were astonished at the array of goods on the shelves. The parents panicked when they realized that they had lost sight of Robert, then about three years old. After searching fruitlessly, Rachel heard Robert sitting amongst the retail goods, "driving" his father's oxen team, Buck and Bright. He had been upset when the team was sold to the new owner of their ranch and was summoning their memory through play. In this game of hiding from his parents, and in the family stories told long afterward about the long trip back from the Prairies, Robert was presented as a clever and spirited little boy, with nothing but talent to distinguish him from other children.

In exploring the bustling city of Winnipeg, Robert John was witnessing the city that his and others' cattle-trade had built. The livestock industry had made Winnipeg into a wealthy city, with Saint Boniface hosting the site of the largest stockyards in the British Empire between 1907 and 1912, precisely when Robert John was developing his skills in livestock herding. By 1910, when Robert John and his family were visiting Winnipeg, twenty-four railway lines radiated from Winnipeg across the Prairies in all directions.[12] Winnipeg must have seemed like the centre of the universe to this rural family.

Little Robert continued to be the centre of attention for his self-confidence and testing of boundaries. After the family reboarded the train out of Winnipeg, it stopped on a siding to let another of the interminable freights pass. Here, Robert fell through the gap between two cars onto the tracks. Frantic screaming brought the conductor running, and he pulled Robert to safety. Accidents like these were probably common on the crowded trains, with parents' attention distracted by the busy environment. These experiences solidified Robert's growing reputation as a risk-taker and as an impish, inquisitive little boy intent on keeping the spotlight on himself.

The family had not only benefitted from the boom years after 1906, but also added to their good fortune by leaving their homestead before the boom went bust in 1913.[13] As an example, while Calgary experienced a major building and population boom from 1906, by 1914, "the bottom washed right out," report Rasporich and Klassen,[14] just as it did in a recession across the rest of the country. With great luck, Robert John and Rachel had perfectly timed their introduction to and exit from homesteading.

On returning to Ontario, the family moved in with Rachel's sister, who lived on a small mixed farm near Grimsby. The host family had two children, and the Killins family now comprised five, but everyone packed into the farmhouse for several months. Moving in temporarily with kin was another common strategy used by families as they became re-established in a new setting. Eventually, Robert John and Rachel found a fruit farm to their liking in the Niagara Peninsula, near to their relatives, but they stayed there only a year. Very likely they rented the farm while they continued to look for one that better fit their needs.

And so continued the pattern of "proving up," where the family expected to buy and sell farms after they had been improved, just as Robert John had done with his homestead in Alberta, and just as former homesteaders were doing right across Canada. Next in the line of farms to be bought and improved was a hundred-acre farm close to Welland, Ontario. Robert John had been impressed by the quality of the out-buildings on the land, and these served him well. But the land had been rented for forty years and was so depleted that the crop yields were low. Here, Robert John began to build a dairy herd, always his first love. He fertilized the land, using both commercial fertilizer and manure from the cattle, and within three years the land was yielding better than any of his neighbours'. This created a new problem which he never solved: finding suitable help to assist with the farm work.

Ever restless, Robert John sold the farm for a good profit. Because his heart problems were increasing, he and Rachel decided that the next move would need to be into town. Robert John took a labouring job in the Shredded Wheat factory in Niagara Falls, Ontario, and found a good house on the outskirts of town with peach, plum, cherry, and pear orchards around the home. There was the obligatory chicken coop as well, large enough to accommodate two dozen chickens. The soil was deemed fertile enough to support extensive vegetable gardens.

The family moved to Niagara Falls in 1914, a town made famous by the Battle of Lundy's Lane in the War of 1812 and by the tourist attraction of the Niagara Falls in the mid-nineteenth century. By 1914, it had a population of about seven thousand, by far the largest centre the family had lived in to date.

The move into town was wrenching for the family, but necessary. The furniture was moved on a hayrack atop the farm wagon by Robert

John and the new owner of the farm. The children had access to better schools in that area, and Rachel was able to find a more satisfying social life with women her age and with her interests. With this, the family embarked on the next stage of their lives, within reach of waged labour for Robert John. At the factory, Robert John held a variety of labouring jobs for some years, after which he became the night watchman. The buying and selling of property would not end with Robert John's employment at the Shredded Wheat factory, however. He would continue periodically buying underperforming farms, hanging on to them for a few years with modest improvements, and then selling them. He was convinced that the route to riches was through buying property; while he never achieved the wealth he sought, the family was comfortable. He also seemed to enjoy this one-man improvement plan. And in the process, he instilled in his children the same goal of speculating in real estate.

Family Dynamics

Once they had moved to Niagara Falls, with Robert John working at the factory and periodically investing in more property, the family settled into a lifestyle determined by Rachel's abiding confidence in education to give her family a better future than she felt her husband's speculation could provide. On weekends, Robert John seems to have been an unusually involved father, taking his sons fishing and working with them in the family's garden.

Rachel's plans for her children included music. The children were provided with mouth organs as a first step in their music education. All of the children were also aware that they were expected to perform well as students, but in this regard as well, Robert was the unrivalled star.

In the little country school attended by the children, Robert quickly attracted the attention of his teachers and the principal, who became a family friend. It is no surprise that Rachel would befriend other educators, and this association might also have added to Robert's social capital. Robert was still in elementary school during the First World War.

He would have studied from a curriculum sanitized of all references to Germans or German culture, except for the study of the German language, which carried on unabated while, for example, music composed by Germans was eliminated from the syllabus.[15] Robert would also have been a member of the school cadet corps, participating in military drill several times a week.

How else were Robert's qualities influenced by the First World War and Canadian public debate of the era? Robert was between seven and twelve when the war raged, and he had no direct relatives involved in the war because of his father's health and age. Further, there was a strong strain of pacifism in the family. And yet, in addition to his experiences at school, Robert would have witnessed the public discourse that willingly stoked anti-German sentiments and condoned casual violence in the community. He would have seen the social dislocation of returning soldiers, maimed physically and mentally, the financial straits of men no longer able to provide for their families, and the hyper-patriotism for Britain and the newly confident Canada after the war.

On entering high school, Robert took the usual courses as well as a variety of subjects in the classics. He was especially lauded for his spatial abilities, giving him an edge in geography, a course he planned to study in university. When he was twelve, he invented a series of improvements for his parents' home, including a "step-down transformer" and plumbing in the family basement. He also became skilled in languages, extending his French studies in his course in "authors and composition" by subscribing to *La Presse* and reading it often to the family. He graduated at the head of his class from high school in 1923.

Thus, when Robert began his studies at Queen's University in 1924, he seemed to have everything he needed for a successful and happy life: a family that admired and supported him, high levels of energy, and demonstrated talent in a variety of fields, as well as the desire to distinguish himself as a leader. But from this point on, Robert also demonstrated a number of troubling qualities: harsh criticism of some authority figures and undue adulation of others, an unwillingness or inability to exercise self-discipline, and a notable lack of social skills, resulting in isolation. He demonstrated strong biases against certain groups, including Germans, and religious denominations. For example, he disparaged evangelical Christians as "ignorant" and Roman Catholics as "benighted," and felt free to savagely criticize anyone on the basis of their lack of knowledge. He had a fascination with guns. And following "country norms," Robert, and indeed the whole family, engaged in casual poking and slapping to get one another's attention. This would not have been regarded as violence in that era, and yet the aggressive physicality was noted by others who did not resort to these displays.

He could become frustrated, and this resulted in explosive anger. This made his university experience uneven and created a significant challenge in the choice of a suitable career. It also created difficulties in sustaining any serious relationships with others, especially women. Accounts exist of public displays of extended screaming as he argued with his sister about some minor matter. It appeared that he had no control over his emotions during these temper tantrums. Afterward, he would reject any suggestion that his reaction had been excessive. It was all a frightening portent for the future.

CHAPTER 2

Two Canadian Families: The Killinses and the Frasers, 1920–1931

During the 1920s, two families lived and raised their children in dramatically different ways. The families were unknown to each other at that time, but their fates would become intertwined from the late 1930s to the 1960s. Each family had three children: two sons and a daughter. One of these children, Robert, would kill his own sister and a member of the other family, Florence Fraser, his estranged wife.

The 1920s was generally characterized by postwar prosperity. Jobs were plentiful, but technology was changing, much of this due to wartime inventions. Many families welcomed the labour-saving devices that were becoming common in the 1920s, including such appliances as ranges and washing machines. Electricity was increasingly common in households as well.

At the same time, the gap between middle-class life and that endured by the poor was growing. The importance of formal education was widely accepted amongst English Canadians as a route to personal satisfaction and economic well-being.

The Killins Siblings

Robert

When Robert arrived at Queen's University in Kingston in 1924 as an undergraduate, he became part of a small elite entering post-secondary education. Even gaining his senior matriculation in high school placed him in a select group in Ontario society at that time. There was a good reason why more students did not proceed beyond grade 8: education was expensive. Finding the money to pay his university fees would have been a stretch for Robert. He took what today we would call a "gap year" after high school, likely to save money for his tuition fees.

Notwithstanding its elite nature, Queen's was a small and struggling university in 1924. With only about fourteen hundred students,[1] Robert could have expected to know many of his classmates, particularly those in his introductory courses. Battered by the First World War, with declining government grants and endowments, and with too few, and poorly paid, professors, the university's academic and social reputation had suffered. By 1924, it was in the shadow of the more robust University of Toronto.

To bolster the flagging fortunes of Queen's, the Dean of Arts O.D. Skelton, who would that year leave to join Mackenzie King's Department of External Affairs in Ottawa, actively recruited new faculty members and worked hard to put his faculty on a firmer footing. During his tenure, Queen's expanded its research capacities, especially to meet the economic and social challenges facing Canada in the postwar era. It also opened new departments in business and public administration. "The days of happy-go-lucky ease, the days when we had a continent to burn are gone for good and all,"[2] Skelton observed.

Due to his and Principal Taylor's fundraising efforts, Queen's was able to burnish its image through a campus facelift: in 1924, the Douglas Library opened with a spacious reading room, administrative offices, and stack-space for three hundred thousand volumes.

The Richardson Football Stadium had recently opened, along with the Jock Harty Arena. In 1925, Lady Byng, the wife of the governor general, opened Ban Righ Hall with accommodation for sixty women students and dining rooms for even more. The endless fundraising was beginning to bear fruit.

Instead of enrolling in one of the new public social science courses that had been opened, Robert was drawn to the classics. He began his university career in a Bachelor of Arts program featuring the standards of history, English, Latin, geology, and French. Studies were important but so, too, was the student social calendar. Like all students, Robert tried to fit in during his classes, but less so through the many social events offered over the opening weeks. He would have had many chances to meet classmates and faculty members as he explored the possibilities of university life.

Queen's offered teams for men to watch and join in football, hockey, basketball, boxing, fencing, and track. In fact, in 1922, hysteria reigned when Queen's defeated the varsity football team from Toronto for the first time in fifteen years.[3] For the more intellectually inclined, one could join an intercollegiate debating team; in fact, they were champions in Robert's first year. An arts society, a dramatic society, the YMCA, an English club, a German club, and "locality clubs" for students from given regions were all available. There was the Queen's student government, which led its members into a general student strike in March 1928 over student rights. There were initiations, dances, and frolics (musical reviews), all giving opportunities to drink, smoke, and talk for hours. But Robert seems to have attended none of these, coming to know no one on a personal level.

He struggled through 1924 and 1925, failing his English course and barely passing his Latin. His marks in his other three courses were undistinguished. Robert had shown that he was both a social outsider and a marginal student, rather than the intellectual hero he had expected to become. His inability and unwillingness to interact with people, his limited academic achievements, and his outsized ego intermingled dangerously for the rest of his life.

The near-failure in his first year shocked Robert. What had happened to his star status in the world? Clearly, his poor performance required some rethinking of his future. He had entered Queen's with the intention of becoming a teacher, but this career now held little attraction. As a seventeen-year-old, his personality was becoming more defined. Teachers require strong social skills to work successfully and happily with students of any age, and it was obvious that Robert lacked much interest in socializing with students his own age and older, much less those who were younger and needed guidance.

Often the brooding scholar was a part of university culture, and Robert was certainly a brooder, and competent in many subjects. But he was also unsettled about his future. Although he was by all accounts intelligent and creative, he lacked patience with others and tended to assert his own ideas noisily and without listening to alternative views. At the same time, despite this blustery shield, he lacked self-discipline in overcoming challenges, giving up quickly. He might very well have experienced depression in this period, his first time away from home, in an environment of competitive intellectualism, and without many satisfying outlets for his reputed energies. Without any doubt, he would have been lonely. No, teaching was not a reasonable career choice. But if not that, what? Dark thoughts must have intruded on his waking days and fretful nights — perhaps he was not cut out for Queen's? Or perhaps, he told himself, he was too good for Queen's. It was not his fault, he reasoned. Others had done him in — students, professors, the university itself.

While he considered his options, both academic and career, he returned home. For the next three years, he helped his father with farm work and learned a bit of carpentry from a local builder. For the rest of his life, he would periodically return to house building as an outlet for his frustrations and as a source of income. But he never worked at carpentry long enough or with enough attention to become a skilled craftsman. Without much sense of order, he would throw together structures without bothering to finish the details. That was left to others, or was not done at all.

Back in the sustaining family circle, he would have re-established the narrative about his superiority, since neither of his siblings appears to have realized that he had come perilously close to failing his first year and ending his university career. We have no evidence of how he explained

Robert as a deeply serious undergraduate in 1931. Graduation photo from Queen's University.

his departure, but we do know that his reputation as the intellectual leader of the family remained intact. It is very likely that explanations he offered in his later life when faced with adversity, for example blaming others for his fate, were first honed in this early period. At the same time, he contributed to the family's welfare, working hard over these three years at a variety of jobs and saving for his tuition costs at Queen's.

Before Robert, now twenty-one years old, returned to his studies in 1928, he wrote to the registrar, requesting a make-up examination in English to "raise his standing." He did well enough on this examination in September to be permitted to carry on with a second-year English course. In a further letter in June 1928, he requested information about changing his major in English and minor in history to a combined course in arts and theology. With this change of majors came the possibility of entering the ministry.

At the same time, he considered transferring his credits to an honours B.A. in English and history, a relatively new option for students, and another program introduced by O.D. Skelton. A pass B.A. required nineteen courses after senior matriculation; the honours B.A. degree required only one more at twenty, but also an oral and written examination on all work completed over the student's years of study.[4] This option would have been most useful if he had been considering a graduate degree, or if he had intended to teach. The honours degree conferred a "specialist" standing in one subject, a higher salary, and prestige in the school system. High school teachers came in large numbers to Queen's after 1918 to qualify for specialist certificates such as this. It is possible that Robert met one or more of these returning teachers as he thought about his own career path. In addition, the new Dean of Arts, John Matheson, was a former high school teacher, as were a number of faculty members of the day, and Robert might well have discussed that profession with them, ultimately rejecting it.

Robert took his full second academic year to decide which degree program he should pursue, and finally, in 1929, he transferred to the combined arts-theology degree, which required four years to complete. Here, he did significantly better, particularly in his theology courses. Winning the Mary Fraser McLennan Prize in Hebrew in May 1929 must have helped him to make up his mind. His record remained uneven, however, with a bare pass in church history in 1930 and a weak mark in public speaking. Both teaching and pastoral work required a good deal of public speaking. Was Robert already second-guessing his choice of theology? His low marks in church history show that he was only partly engaged in the discipline[5]. He seemed to like the idea of speaking to his flock, or at least being in a position of authority to air his many views.

Furthermore, there is no evidence that Robert attended church while in Kingston. The official transcript has a blank next to the request of the name of his "church in Kingston." This certainly was not because there were too few churches from which to choose! Kingston had many churches close to the university, including Methodist, his family's denomination. In deciding not to commit himself to one church or denomination, Robert demonstrated his limited interest in religion generally. It also showed that he disregarded the importance of a single church's culture, something he would ultimately be responsible for as a minister of that church.

In this period, too, Robert developed a worrying tendency to hoard, especially reading material, which was soon stacked up in whatever bedroom he was occupying at a given time. He was increasingly untidy in his living arrangements, where goods were strewn about, dishes remained unwashed, and clutter covered all surfaces. Academic types have often found a space for oddness or eccentricity in the university, but Robert's messy living spaces seemed to indicate a scattered and even discombobulated mind.

Balanced against these personality oddities was genuine kindness for his family and relatives. He wrote daily to his brother while the latter was at university, forging a loyal relationship that would last a lifetime; he took on construction jobs for his sister and accepted little pay for these. His explanation for this was that he had a skill of building and he would offer it to those he loved. He consistently sought out those who were marginalized in society and did what he could to assuage poverty. For several summers during his university studies, he worked in the "mission field" in northern Ontario with marginalized Franco-Ontarians, making good use of his French. This likely involved offering church services and some pastoral work. And he was hungry for new ideas. He listened to the radio and attended lectures throughout his life to absorb and criticize them.

Robert had developed a personality that was at once combative, intolerant, and undisciplined, while at the same time demonstrating loyalty and kindness to some. He was not unsympathetic to the problems of others. He chose not to participate in a church community or socialize with people, and when forced to do so he was awkward and uncomfortable. But he did take his spiritual journey seriously and remained a lifelong learner. He became a droning lecturer but not a collegial conversationalist who listened, responded, and asked questions. He appeared to lack what today we would term social intelligence.

He had completed a university degree that seemed to qualify him for a single profession: that of a minister of the Church. The fact that his options were very limited suggests that his decision-making was flawed in having created a lone path for himself, a path that concluded with a career for which he was not suited.

In terms of his ideas, Robert was a man of his era. Like many left-leaning reformers, his views reflected those of the social-democratic Cooperative Commonwealth Federation Party (CCF), which had been organized in 1932. Nevertheless, Robert's political and social views were a study in contrasts. He was far from a consistent thinker. While a supporter of unions and the rights of men in the workplace, he had no interest in getting to know these workers. He believed the cooperative movement would bring greater equality to society, while at the same time he was an elitist. He was a temperance advocate of the shrill variety, castigating anyone who enjoyed alcohol, while at the same time rejecting the anti-patriarchal principles of many temperance advocates. He was anti-monarchist but found the "common man" repulsive; he was a pacifist and yet engaged in violent arguments that often ended in physical altercations. He loved guns. Robert enjoyed the backwoods and hunting, and yet he felt superior to country folk, never forging real friendships with anyone in the country, either in this period or later.

Robert had long allied himself with other violent protesters. In the 1920s, when still a young man, he was an active member of the Ku Klux Klan. Whether he marched on racialized people's lawns with a pillowcase over his head is not known, but he both feared and detested people of colour. He allowed his membership to lapse by the 1930s, but he certainly did not jettison his racist views and his penchant for violence.

Amongst his most hated enemies were Roman Catholics. In this, Robert was also representative of his age. Throughout all of the nineteenth and much of the twentieth centuries in Canada, there was little common ground between Protestants and Catholics. Education, politics, civic duties, charitable endeavours — all had Catholic and Protestant versions in their communities so that supporters of one faith rarely met those of the other. Robert was a proud member of the Loyal Orange Institution, or what is commonly called the Orange Order. He took pleasure in marching on July 12 in the Orange Order Parades and in assuming the worst of any Catholic. In his mind, all Catholics were stupid, clannish, unable to think for themselves, and even disloyal citizens, offering their loyalty first to their Pope and only afterward to their country. The range of epithets he used on Catholics included Papists, Dogans, and Romish. He had an inexhaustible and, by today's standards, adolescent well of hostility toward Catholics.

Gladys

By the early 1920s, Gladys had experimented with several jobs, none of which had produced a clear way forward. She had graduated from senior matriculation in high school (grade 12) in 1917 and had her sights on city life. Just fifteen years old, her goal at this time was to be a self-supporting artist. But lack of capital made this an impossible choice. The 1921 census lists her as "employed" but offers no details. With few alternatives presenting themselves to a young woman seeking to be independently employed, Gladys chose the practical route of teaching. At the age of twenty-two, she attended Normal school with the aim of becoming an art teacher and began teaching when she was twenty-three. At this age, she would have been older than many of her female teaching colleagues.

Gladys obtained a teaching position at the newly opened Memorial Elementary School in Niagara Falls, Ontario, in 1924. Thus, while she had not made the leap to the city as she had hoped, she was at least a "townie" and able to live a more cosmopolitan life.

By now, she had matured into a woman with definite ideas that she felt free to express, a strong sense of her own abilities, a sharper analysis of the failings of others, and a loathing of children and youths. Despite having received a first-class teaching certificate in 1936, and

A selection from Gladys's Royal Crown Derby Blue Mikado tea set.

an art supervisor's certificate in 1937, which would have increased her pay (today, this would be called a specialist's certificate in art), she hated teaching and was impatient with the students who came with her career. So many were disinterested and disobedient; she faced continual disappointment and frustration.

Like her brother, Gladys adopted left-leaning ideas throughout the 1920s, supporting the rise of communism in Russia and reading widely to support her political and social leanings. Like Robert, she was impatient with the poorly educated, with those who disparaged artistic expressions, and with the limitations on women's public lives. She celebrated women's right to vote, won in the previous decade, and took a deep interest in public policies. And, like Robert, she preferred to talk rather than to listen, raising her voice and ire when countered. With her experience in education, she was comfortable in lecturing to anyone who would listen.

Although the demands of teaching in these early years did not offer her much time for her own work, she did devote increasing energies to the study of art. None of her paintings from the 1920s survive, although we know she practiced her art then. In this period, her chosen subjects were often interior still lifes.

Ada Gladys Killins.

Gladys seems to not have liked her fellow teachers much better than the students, and she failed to make any lasting friendships with her teaching colleagues. Her isolation as a teacher is striking. Her unhappiness with teaching is understandable, given her rigid and demanding personality and the specificity of her subject matter, in which few students excelled. Gladys seemed unable to engage students without much artistic talent. Since the point of strong pedagogy is to do just that, we must conclude that Gladys was not a natural teacher, nor one who benefitted from the instruction she would have received from Normal school, nor even one who learned her craft in the classroom, as many teachers do.

Despite the fact that she enjoyed neither her students nor her colleagues, she spent the next twenty-three years at the same school. It is surprising that she did not consider moving schools or applying to one of the continuation schools, which had classes up to grade 10 — for which she was qualified — and a more mature student clientele than she would have endured at her public school assignment.

Having a steady income, albeit at work she did not like, and a peer group of other employed women, Gladys developed a relatively satisfying life with the trappings of culture. In the 1920s, Gladys purchased a fine china tea set in the Royal Crown Derby Blue Mikado pattern, one that was very popular for that period in Ontario. In this apparent bid for conventionality and a refined life, Gladys ensured that her tea set also had a special cigarette dish for her guests. Once finished their tea, the ladies would be invited to light up their cigarettes in this era of yet unparalleled female emancipation and tobacco consumption by modern young women. Gladys remained a heavy smoker throughout her life.

In her bid to develop a sophisticated image, Gladys showed that she could be engaging and supportive to those she found compatible. Letters between her and her brother's father-in-law, Alpheus Fry, an intellectual and educated farmer, demonstrate the bond between them. Her active letter-writing program with her family and with people she admired during the 1920s to the 1940s supports an identity of a worldly woman, well versed in current affairs and thoughtful about spiritual issues.

Harold

Rachel was one of those mothers who had favourites amongst her children, and Harold, last born and slow to develop, was not her favourite. Interestingly, however, he was the most loyal of the children, staying on the farm with his parents throughout the 1920s and 1930s, until their deaths, after he had graduated with junior matriculation (grade 11). At sixteen, he was carrying much of the load of farm work as his father's health declined. But Harold could not manage all 147 acres on his own, and in 1925, it was decided that the farm would need to be sold, with the family moving back to Niagara Falls. Harold carried the guilt with him for years that he could not run the farm entirely on his own, and Rachel at least — if not Robert John — allowed him to imagine that a stronger and more able sixteen-year-old would have been able to supply everything that the farm needed.

Within two years, the family made its final move to a farm in Fonthill, Ontario. By this time, in 1927, Harold was running the farm alone at the age of eighteen and keeping about three hundred colonies of bees. The beekeeping business he ran sustained the farm operation for years and seeded Harold's academic interest in apiary culture.

Not even his successful beekeeping business and maintaining the farm in the face of his father's precarious health warmed Rachel to Harold, however. One wonders what he would have had to do to effectively compete in her mind with his older siblings. Whatever it would have taken, he did not do it, and he continued to live in the shadow of brilliant Robert and artistic Gladys.

In 1928, Harold decided that he would return to school. But before doing so, he resolved to sign on with one of the Western Canadian harvest excursions, where young men from eastern Canada were paid to take the train west to work on huge wheat farms when the crops were harvested in mid- and late summer. This trip proved to be a turning point for him, and for the West, too: it was the last of the harvest excursions before the dust bowl of the Great Depression put an end to most crops of any kind.

Harold happened to have an uncle, one of Rachel's brothers, Uncle Edgar, who had a farm near Lucky Lake, Saskatchewan. To say that Harold revelled in the hard work of harvesting, and the comradeship of the many other young men who had signed on from Ontario and the Maritimes, is an understatement. He raved about the experience for the rest of his long life. This trip, the first that Harold had taken anywhere, returned him to the landscape of his birth in 1909 on that homestead in Mannville, Alberta. The Saskatchewan spread he worked on was similar to what he had heard about his father's homesteading. He could not get enough of it, taking pictures and keeping journals throughout the summer. It seeded a lifelong admiration for western Canada and local Indigenous Peoples. He collected and framed photographs of Indigenous Chiefs that he treasured throughout his life.

On the spread where he was harvesting, Harold met a young man interested in travelling farther west after the harvest was in. With him, he took the train to Prince Rupert. He snapped photograph after photograph with his Kodak Brownie and remembered the camaraderie with his friend on this identity-forming trip before his first year of university.

In the fall of 1928, Harold, then nineteen years old, entered the Ontario Agricultural College (OAC) at Guelph, now the University of Guelph. He took advantage of the associate course, which allowed candidates to complete the final two years of their high school and a two-year agricultural program leading to a bachelor of science in agriculture degree, also called a B.S.A.

This was the same year that Robert returned to Queen's, and Harold must have reflected on the difficulty of the years before him. Like Robert, he was responsible for finding money for his own tuition fees. Harold cheerfully worked in the kitchen and at serving the other students in the dining hall to earn his passage, and reportedly loved doing it. In his final year, he received a scholarship to defray his expenses as he worked on his honours' thesis on the culture of bees.

In 1931, Harold had completed his senior matriculation and had been accepted into the B.S.A. program under the auspices of the University of Toronto. The fact that this achievement — from the slow-learning baby of the family — was virtually ignored by his parents did not blunt the satisfaction he felt in having earned the senior matriculation qualifier.

Like his adored brother and sister, Harold held to a left-leaning analysis of Canadian society. He attended meetings of the United Farmers of Ontario and supported their platform completely. He also admired Russian Communism, as did his siblings, and for a time, took out membership in the Canadian Communist Party. Later, he would become a member of the Cooperative Commonwealth Federation and, later yet, work during elections on behalf of the New Democratic Party.

Somehow, he escaped the blight of Ontario Protestantism in ridiculing Roman Catholicism. He was remarkably ecumenical in his religious views, with an interest in Buddhism, Hinduism, and even Spiritualism. A member of the United Church of Canada, he prided himself on being a thorn in its side in reminding them of the social gospel mission that characterized the United Church in the 1920s, urging them at the general council to again take up the mantle of social activism on behalf of the dispossessed.

Like the rest of his family, he loved a good debate and engaged in discussion often. But here, again, he differed in that he had learned the value of listening to his interlocutors. How had he done this when his siblings and mother were content to present their views at an ever-louder volume but without engaging others? Perhaps it was his OAC experience, perhaps his stronger social relations with others.

But it was in personality structure that Harold was most different from his siblings. Where Robert and Gladys were aggressive and combative in debate, he was gentle. He was prepared to lose these supper-table arguments, too, perhaps because he had lost so many as the youngest child. Where both Robert and Gladys were increasingly cynical, Harold was endlessly optimistic. There was no situation that seemed catastrophic on the face of it in which he would not find a silver lining. In this way, he was much more like his father than his caustic mother, who set the tone for family discourse. At home, Harold's views were often discounted because of his optimism, as if a positive view was simple-minded. But this did not discourage his world view, and he seemed to enjoy being known for his sunny ways while the rest of the family indulged in Eeyore-like grumbling.

One of Harold's classmates, Samuel Fry, invited him to his home one weekend in their first year. There he met Samuel's sister, Harriet Ethel, called Ethel by the family. Ethel was about to enter nursing training. The attraction was immediate, and they dated for about a year. Ethel ultimately ended the relationship because she felt that Harold was too short for her. Ethel was a willowy five-foot-nine beauty, and Harold was perhaps five foot four when standing on his toes. "I knew that I would never be able to wear high heels," explained Ethel. Social norms limit our choices in strange ways.

Thus, by 1931, all three of the Killins siblings had either graduated or were pursuing higher education from Normal school to university. Given their modest origins, this was a remarkable educational achievement, testifying to the resolve with which their mother had raised them, and the ability of the young people themselves to meet her high standards.

The Frasers

The Fraser family came to know the Killins family through the marriage of their daughter, Florence, to Robert Killins in 1938. The families had very little in common and, eventually, neither did Robert and Florence. In the 1920s, the couple had not yet met; however, the family history predates their association.

Ira and Pearl Viola Fraser, parents of Florence, married in June 1915, before Ira joined the Canadian Expeditionary Force in November that year. Pearl Viola, (called Pearly by her family) felt that she had married down, a fact that she never allowed her husband to forget. In virtually every important aspect of life, from religion to family income to professional status, Pearl Viola's family trumped her husband's. While this probably did not matter when they wed, this fact soon divided the couple and eventually created a chasm between them.

Pearly, born in 1894, was the sixth child of nine to Mary and Frederich Thomas. Her family was descended from German immigrants and held strictly to Presbyterianism. Her father was a teacher in Waterloo, Ontario. We can safely assume that Pearly herself had considerably more education and common sense than did Ira, her hapless husband. Pearly was serious and battled throughout her married life to maintain respectability.

Florence's father, Ira Alexander (at an early age, called Ira Allan) Fraser, from Wittenberg, Colchester County, Nova Scotia, was a charmer. Born in 1892,[6] Ira was raised in a second family created from the marriage of his widowed mother, Margaret Sibley, and Frederick Fraser. Ira seems not to have had a warm relationship with his stepfather. The story he told of his youth was that, as a result of his unhappiness, he left home at the age of twelve and found a job with the railway. However, the 1911 census shows him still at home at eighteen, working as a fireman on the railway. Perhaps he left and returned to the household, as was common with many young working men of that era. In these early years, Ira suffered a crush injury to his foot, resulting in the loss of that foot's arch. He was employed by the Canadian Pacific Railway (CPR) for some fifty years. He started as a fireman, a gruelling job that involved shovelling coal into the boilers of the locomotive. Gradually he worked his way up to engineer. For many years, however, his jobs were low-skilled and poorly paid.

Pearl Viola and Ira were warring parents. By all accounts, the children were close, continuing to enjoy each other's company into adulthood. Perhaps they banded together and found solace in one another because their parents' marriage was deeply dysfunctional. The children were party to high levels of discord in the household.

Almost immediately on entering war service in 1915, Ira experienced an unfortunate accident. While in England, he was kicked in the groin by a horse. While he was not hospitalized for this injury, he suffered pain from it over the course of the war and probably for years afterward.

Within two weeks of his arrival in England he was admitted to hospital and treated for suspected gonorrhea. There were no antibiotics to treat sexually transmitted diseases, so the bladder irrigations with potassium permanganate were very hard on him. He was readmitted for a second treatment a month later and then a third time in June of 1915, whereupon a diagnosis of syphilis was made. This was described in the records as a recurrence of an infection he had acquired six years previously. The treatment was twofold: arsphenamine (which is an arsenic compound) and mercury topical cream. These treatments took months. He was finally discharged from hospital in August 1915. He was also found to have an inflamed appendix, a swollen testicle (from the horse injury), and his one flat foot.

It appears that Ira's extended hospitalization was caused by the first two treatments having failed due to misdiagnosis. On his return from overseas, Ira was assessed for possible disability related to the testicular injury from the horse. He was found to have a hydrocele (a cystic swelling) associated with a testicle that was atrophying. Surgery was suggested, which would have involved removing the cyst and testicle, but Ira declined. No disability pension was given to him.

When he was fit enough to be in the field, he played the trumpet in the battalion bugle band. This would have required Ira to play at many

Pearl Viola Fraser.

military funerals, sad and depressing events for a young man away from home for the first time. Ira clearly found his war service to have been unpleasant. He reported to his grandchildren that he and his musician buddies had thrown their instruments overboard on the ship home, never playing again. This was their gesture of leaving the horrors of the war behind forever.

Pearl Viola gave birth to her first child in 1916 while Ira was serving overseas. She was left to care for their infant son, George, alone on the meagre salary of what a soldier voluntarily set aside for his family. It was usually half his pay — around fifteen or twenty dollars a month — but even the full amount would not have been enough for her to live comfortably. She returned to her family in Waterloo, where she became reacquainted with a better standard of living and conversation. This created a chronic hearkening back throughout her life to the more gracious lifestyle of her parents and siblings in comparison to her hardscrabble existence with Ira. Her nostalgia mixed with her mounting anger at Ira's inability to measure up to her relatives.

Pearl Viola became increasingly religious and censorious of moral lapses, mainly Ira's. Her husband would provide much evidence that she was morally superior to him; in fact, she felt herself more virtuous than most people. When Pearl Viola discovered that, between his treatments for venereal diseases, her husband had found the time to father at least one son while overseas, all her fears about his moral laxity were confirmed.

On Ira's return in 1919 when he was twenty-seven, he fell even further under Pearl Viola's shadow, acting as a kind of bystander as she ran the family. She had done so during the lean war years, and there seemed no good reason to let go of the reins with the return of her husband. But they were not entirely estranged, and Florence Irene's birth in 1920 stretched the family's resources even further. When William joined the siblings in 1924, the family was close to abject poverty.

Ira's ability and willingness to provide for his family was limited, partly because, at that time, railway employees were so poorly paid and partly, too, because he did not always turn over his full pay to his wife, reserving something for his own pleasures. The children recounted Ira being locked out of the house for his infractions, usually over-indulgent drinking, and spending nights on the back porch.

Ira's war experience seems to have instilled in him a rough masculinity, common in those men who suffered both physically and emotionally in their wartime service. Certainly, Ira's positive qualities — his lightheartedness, sense of humour, and work ethic — were much more appreciated by the males around him than by women. The latter often found him clumsy and inarticulate and, of course, much in Pearl Viola's shade. Whether or not Ira deserved his wife's fierce judgments of his behaviour, he did not present a model of a loving husband to his children. Was Florence seeking to escape him and the circumstances of her family life?

Ira Fraser.

The family lived in deplorably poor quarters close to the tracks. To make ends meet, the children became proficient thieves, stealing from farmers' fields to provide their mother with vegetables for a weak stew. They also recalled the house being so cold in winter that everyone slept in the kitchen while wearing as many clothes as they could, with blankets slung on the walls to keep the frost at bay. Christmas passed without gifts or even enough food. One of the children had rickets, a bone disease caused by malnutrition, and lacked shoes for school. At one point, the family was so short of food and clothing that Florence called a charity

George, Florence, and William George Fraser in the mid-1930s. Despite deep poverty, the Fraser children were close and remained on positive terms throughout their lives.

to request hampers for a "poor family," which turned out to be her own. She got the supplies they needed and never looked back. These life skills would come in handy later in her own marriage.

The Fraser children were younger than the Killins children. A very different ethos operated in their family life from that of the Killinses, who were driven and competitive. By 1931, George was fifteen, Florence was eleven, and Bill was seven. All remained in school when they had the clothing to attend, but there was no pressure for any of them to excel in academics. The Frasers lived in Winnipeg, and had it not been for a visit

Florence paid to northern Ontario, the families would likely never have met. But meet they did, with catastrophic results.

Nevertheless, the children did have happy times, often exploring the outdoors or engaging in activities that did not require money. In the above photograph of the three siblings playing in a stream, Florence's fresh beauty is on display in her carefree play with her brothers.

Ira and Pearl Viola had a marriage filled with frustration and anger, with the atmosphere in the house thick with retribution and insults. Of the three siblings in Ira and Pearl Viola's family, Florence was unquestionably the most sociable and outgoing. She drew this from her father, who was an approachable and easygoing model. George was dutiful and responsible and gave emotional support to Florence throughout her life. William was coddled and protected by their mother as the baby. Florence was bright, inventive, pretty, and flirtatious.

This, then, was the fractious family within which Florence matured. She would have taken several lessons from her family life: first, that many marriages were unhappy, but that the partners had no choice but to endure them; secondly, that a resilient woman could keep a family going in hard times and in good and that a family's welfare was directly linked to the woman's resourcefulness; and thirdly, that for the sake of the children, a mother must persist in any domestic arrangement, unless it was completely untenable. She had no models of a wife running away from an unhappy home life. The mentoring she had received was of a wife making do in an unhappy union, with her pride in persevering despite adversity.

By 1931, this tale of two families demonstrates that the Killinses were moving into the modern era through careful family and personal investments in land and education. The other family, the Frasers, held to an older prescription of a lifestyle rooted in manual labour. While this allowed for subsistence living, it did not permit the family to take advantage of the general prosperity in the country. Those differences would become accentuated in the next decades.

CHAPTER 3

Pursuing New Paths: The 1930s

————

The era of the Great Depression encompassed, surprisingly, some of the best years for Robert, Gladys, and Harold, as well as Florence and her brothers: Robert was starting his ministry and was full of hope; Gladys was an established teacher and had embarked on her career as a water-colourist; Harold graduated university and found love during this decade and married his sweetheart; Florence left school at seventeen and married the next year; George and William both eventually found jobs with the CPR. All of these young people were building their careers and personal lives, searching for love and success. It was an optimistic stage in all their lives, full of potential and promise.

Robert, now twenty-four years old in May 1931, graduated with his B.A. in arts and theology. During these perilous economic times, there were not a lot of career choices for someone with Robert's credentials. Ordained by the Toronto Conference of the United Church of Canada in 1932, Robert became a minister in the largest Protestant denomination in Canada. The United Church had about 2,240,000 adherents at the time of church union in 1925[1]. Union had been created by the amalgamation of the Methodist, Congregationalist, and local Union churches and about 70 percent of the Presbyterian adherents in Canada.[2] In the late 1950s, about 20 percent of the Canadian population belonged to the United Church of Canada.[3]

Church union had been the solution to a host of problems faced by the four denominations in an era of secularism and seemingly needless competition for resources and souls. By 1925, many Protestant denominations had been reduced to a fraction of their earlier size. As an amalgamated denomination, the goal of the United Church had been to shape "the moral ethos of Canadian society by infusing the values of Evangelical British Protestantism into Canadian citizens and society through evangelism, Christian education, social service, public activism, and advocacy."[4] Given his personal history, Robert would have been a supporter of all of these objectives of the new United Church. But acting on them was another matter.

Even with the financial and social strains created by the Great Depression, the United Church of Canada generally remained strongly supported by its parishioners. In 1935, at the height of the Depression, the tenth anniversary of the creation of the United Church brought out fifteen thousand congregants to celebrate at the Maple Leaf Gardens in Toronto.[5] In fact, it has been argued that the Depression helped to bind the young United Church together as no period of prosperity would have done.[6] However, in local congregations, there was often deep distress and poverty.

With the Canadian economic system in decline, churches that had never been prosperous were hit especially hard. Some United Church congregations were unable to pay their ministers in full or at all. Additional pressure was applied to central presbyteries (who controlled the hiring of ministers for individual congregations) to take in ministers from other denominations, for example, from the Baptists, many of whom were poor before the Depression and were now indigent.

Just what did a minister in the 1930s and '40s do? To begin, most ministers were male; the first woman to be ordained in the United Church was Lydia Emelie Gruchy in 1936, but it would be many years before women ministers were common or accepted. For guidance as to the job description, we might draw on the records of another United Church minister of that period, the Rev. Dr. Peter Anderson of MacKay United Church in Ottawa. He remained in his parish from 1904 until 1934 and was a revered leader in both his community and congregation.

His records at MacKay United Church show that there were three general areas of responsibility. First, ministers were expected to administer their own churches with the help of the church council.[7] The minister operated as an ex-officio member of the council to ensure responsible policies and behaviours in the church operations. The minister was a compulsory member of the presbytery, which was the collection of churches in a given area, and ministers represented their congregations at the presbytery's regular meetings, accepting membership on committees at that level.

Secondly, the minister's religious leadership in the local congregation meant engagement in regular pastoral care of congregants who needed spiritual support. This might involve visiting the sick and elderly, ensuring that they had adequate and nourishing food, and mobilizing other church members to provide a supportive community. They carried out infant baptisms, mentoring the parents and extended family in their responsibilities for the child's spiritual development, and they performed weddings for members of the church. They organized and held Communion for the congregation. Funerals would have been held and burial arrangements made for interment in the churchyard. Youth education was under his authority, often with a Sunday school superintendent to find suitable teachers for the children in Sunday school and older children in the youth societies. And, of course, the minister researched and wrote weekly sermons and delivered them on Sunday mornings, or, if there were several congregations under his watch requiring itinerant service, at some point that day.

Third, at the community level, the minister expected to be called upon in times of stress or crisis to provide moral leadership. Rev. Dr. Anderson, for example, testified in the case of a Chinese boy who was not associated with his church but who was believed to have been abused by his uncles who ran a local laundry. He was instrumental in having the boy removed from his uncles' care and placed with a family who sheltered him. At the same time, Rev. Dr. Anderson regularly worked with the local physician to comfort the sick and dying. He also engaged in fundraising for worthy community causes.

From 1932 with Robert's first posting in White River, Ontario, until his last appointment in Clanwilliam, Bertle Presbytery, in Manitoba in 1943, it was clear that Robert was not well suited to be a successful small-town minister of the United Church. His arguments with the Church councils, his unwillingness to work with people on committees at either his pastoral charge or the presbytery levels, his lacklustre performance in the pulpit, and his apparent misunderstanding of the pastoral labour central to the ministry all marked him as someone who either did not understand his role, or who rejected it. None of this is surprising, since Robert had demonstrated few of the qualities needed to be an admired and productive minister when he studied at Queen's. He might have grown into his duties, but he did not.

Nevertheless, things started out reasonably well in all his charges. The novelty alone must have been invigorating. He was named to four charges over the course of his career with the United Church, three in northern Ontario and one in northern Manitoba. Each posting was poorer than the last one, all of them caught in the deepening Depression. In three out of the four cases, he fought with the church council about his duties, salary, housing, and probably doctrine, although the latter is not recorded in the church records.

The pattern of his service became predictable: Robert would begin with high hopes for his role in the new parish, often offering to lead a committee's work. Then he would start lodging complaints and appeals. He demanded money from every level: the church council, the presbytery,[8] and likely the national church organization, when none had any. He seems to have ignored the fact that a depression was impoverishing the land. The minute books show that he was turned down every time, with surprise expressed by the authorities at the amount Robert requested, or that he was requesting at all. Next, he would recede into surly silence, ignoring whatever few responsibilities he had accepted, and missing meetings or remaining obstinately unresponsive if he did attend. Finally, Robert would look around for another, presumably better posting, request it, and leave.

From White River in the Algoma Presbytery, near what is today Pukaskwa National Park,[9] to Cartier, near Sudbury, to Depot Harbour, near Parry Sound, and finally to Clanwilliam, near Minnedosa in Manitoba, Robert moved from poor to almost destitute postings as the anticipated wealthy parish where he would be admired and paid handsomely slipped further from his grasp.

Never sympathetic to Indigenous people, Robert found increasing numbers amongst his parishioners. In fact, in his third posting at Depot Harbour, the townsite had been built on an Anishinaabe reserve. A loophole in the Indian Act allowed Indigenous people to sell portions of reserve land for railway expansion. J.R. Booth, the Ottawa lumber magnate, took advantage of this and bought 127 hectares of land from the Anishinaabe, creating the town of Depot Harbour as a settlement within the reserve. Booth wanted to use the town as a shipping and rail centre for his timber. By the time Robert arrived there in 1940, many townsfolk had abandoned their homes, and Depot Harbour became almost a ghost town as a result of the Depression and fewer products being shipped out, leaving the Anishinaabe to be a significant percentage of the townsfolk and United Church membership.

All the parishes were in beautiful, natural settings. The area had also been immortalized by the Group of Seven.[10] One has only to think of the vibrant colours in Tom Thomson's paintings of the region to appreciate its unending beauty. However, while living in an area replete with forests, lakes, and rivers would have fit Robert's inclinations, the parish's social needs were great, and any anticipated intellectual comradeship was absent.

Despite the natural beauty of the parishes' settings, Robert did not thrive in the locations or as a minister. He seems to have consistently read his congregations and church councils poorly, either misunderstanding what was needed or refusing to comply with their requests. One example of how completely Robert misunderstood his role concerns the community service he was expected to provide. In a letter from 1938 when he was serving in Cartier, he notes that

> a woman at Levack applied for a child to adopt from the Children's Aid Society. They wrote to me and asked me whether she would be all right to look after it. Some people think she is a trifle crazy as she tried to commit suicide last year. She fired two 38-revolver shots right through herself but got over it entirely. It might be a trifle hard on a baby.[11]

The tone of this letter is unmistakably cynical, making an attempt at humour about a depressed woman wanting to adopt a child after having attempted suicide. While we do not learn of his final assessment, it seems likely that he did not speak on behalf of the woman in this case, but rather made fun of her. That the case was referred to him at all demonstrates that he was expected to serve as a community resource. How different this scenario is from the one of the Rev. Dr. Anderson of MacKay United Church in Ottawa who saved the Chinese boy from abuse.

Occasionally, Robert accepted a task that he genuinely enjoyed. In 1938, he was selected by the presbytery to be the "press reporter," or the contact between the presbytery and local newspapers. He acquitted himself well enough that he was reappointed the next year to the same position. In April 1938 he wrote to his father that "two fellows came who put the news in the Sudbury paper and kept me talking for about an hour." This would have provided Robert with informed journalists with whom to talk and an outlet for his views, which were increasingly racist and anti-Catholic. In the same letter he writes that "[Premier] Hepburn claims he is not going to give the Dogans anything but the chances are he will."[12] One wonders if in these exchanges Robert glimpsed another, more satisfying career — that of a journalist.

Another pattern emerged in his parishes when one would have expected to find a celebration. The churches' council minutes show that despite the hard times, the congregations usually found the resources to celebrate a minister's induction, notice of leaving, or some other noteworthy event, such as the anniversary of a minister's ordination in the church. A ceremony would be arranged with a luncheon following it, prepared by the United Church women and served in the hall. But in Robert's case, his inductions were ignored; his arrivals and departures were quiet and unheralded.[13] Perhaps the Depression had so eaten into the parishioners' incomes that there was little left for a party. More than likely — since these luncheons and teas always involved home-cooking and food from many hands — the council liked their minister so little from the very start that they simply sidestepped the usual hospitality.

Florence and her brother William, late 1930s.

William, Florence, and George, 1943.

Why did Robert move so often? Many ministers, such as the noted Rev. Dr. Anderson in Ottawa, stayed in one parish for their entire career. One possible explanation is that Robert's personal life took a dramatic turn in 1938. A pretty young woman, Florence Fraser, caught his eye. Florence was seventeen; he was thirty-one. In this, Florence was in step with the national average, while Robert was far behind. The age of marital partners declined during and after the war.[14]

The whirlwind romance seems to have begun when Florence, who lived with her family in Winnipeg, was visiting relatives in Cartier, where Robert had his charge. Her mother's brother, who was visually impaired, Uncle Leslie [Wilford] Thomas, was also visiting Cartier from Waterloo, and he offered to be a guest organist in the church where Robert served. Leslie was Florence's favourite uncle, and she tried to see him as often as possible. Florence attended church both to hear her uncle perform and for the service itself, meeting Robert in the process.

In the photograph on page 61, we see Florence ready for a hike with her brother Bill. In the photograph above, she stands before a car with

Florence, Ira, and Pearl, 1944.

her brothers, hugging both. Her brothers were handsome, athletic young men, much like their father, if with a much stronger sense of responsibility than he had. Florence enjoyed the company of her brothers throughout her life.

Pearl Viola's hopes for her daughter Florence were high: she would amount to something if she married well, as Pearl Viola asserted often and loudly. Florence was much closer to her mother than to her feckless father, belying the cozy family scene of Ira holding Florence's first child, baby Pearl, at the train yards in the above photograph.

Ira remained a handsome charmer into his fifties. Ira did not give Florence a good example of a devoted family man, but she also resisted the oppressive religiosity of her mother. Pearl Viola struggled to maintain appearances of respectability in the face of a wandering husband and too little money. Florence did remain conventionally religious, even though she rejected what she regarded as the excesses of her mother's faith system. She taught Sunday school, both before and after her marriage. She distrusted her father's easy charm: perfect for portraits but ineffective for sustaining a family. Above all, Florence wanted to escape her fractious and poor family as well as her boring life in Winnipeg. By her own admission, she was a rebellious teenager. She had completed grade 10, but before she could acquire any job-related training, her mother forced her to stay at home. Without money or education, no escape would be possible other than by marrying up the social ladder, as Pearl Viola commanded.

Meeting Robert Killins, the United Church minister in Cartier, Ontario, was exciting for both Florence and her mother, who put great store in the dignity of church clergy. Florence and Robert began an

Robert and Florence, 1938.

awkward courtship in 1938. The relationship seems to have developed quickly, with Florence waiting until she was eighteen to marry Robert.

From the start, Robert treated Florence like a child, correcting her grammar, telling her where to go and who to see, always the one in charge of the relationship. He was adamant that he did not want children, because Florence was his child-bride. This should have rung some danger bells for Florence and her family, but both Florence and her mother were star-struck with the prospect of marriage to a minister of the Church. Her father barely noticed what was happening. And given her younger age, her lesser status in the community, and the norms of the era, Robert's demands would not have been regarded as unusual.

In the above photograph, likely an engagement picture, the couple sits compatibly enough, although oddly separate. With her carefully coiffed hair and her modest dress, Florence looks radiant in her youth and happiness. Robert, too, looks settled and younger than his years.

The thirteen-year difference in the ages of Robert and Florence was mirrored by many other mismatches in their relationship. Florence had little formal education while Robert had a university degree; Florence had been raised in poverty and, while Robert's family was not wealthy, his family had become comfortably situated as landed farmers and all three children had attained post-secondary education. Robert had a much more fragile identity than did Florence in that he had not experienced the success he had hoped for, either in university or in the pulpit; Florence was clearer about what she wanted in life: a happy family, some entertainment, and enough money to support herself and her children. Robert's needs were more complex and difficult to fulfill; he wanted the admiration of others within an established institution like the United Church of Canada.

But there were also a good number of similarities, which made them potentially compatible and representative of many Canadians in the late 1930s and early 1940s: both came from households where a demanding and more educated mother dominated family culture and ideals; both held traditional notions of men's and women's familial roles, although Florence would have had a stronger example on which to draw as a wife

Robert and Florence Killins on their wedding day, 1938.

who kept the family afloat; both valued religion as an institution, with relatively less importance accorded to individual spiritual growth. While Florence was desperate to escape an unhappy family life and eager to establish her own household, Robert, too, was seeking security and a more established domestic life. There was good reason at the start of their relationship to assume that this marriage would be as happy as many.

There is some evidence that Robert hid their relationship. There is no mention of their marriage in the church records, for example, nor did he comment on it in regular letters to his family. The marriage on December 28, 1938, occurred in the busy Christmas season. Robert and Florence were married in Sudbury by a United Church colleague, with two witnesses, one of whom was the wife of the attending minister. No one from his congregation attended, and no members of either family. How can we explain this? The silence around this major life decision, particularly for a thirty-one-year-old parish minister, is striking. At the very least, it suggests that the marriage was not a result of long planning, nor of careful consideration by either partner. It was not a union discussed with family or any friends the couple might have made in the community. It also gives the impression of the marriage being a clandestine act. This was especially so for Robert, and Florence might have agreed to this, as she agreed to everything in the early years.

The wedding picture for Robert and Florence shows them standing awkwardly apart, as if they are uncomfortable in each other's presence. Robert sits, as in photographs and images of patriarchs from the past, while Florence stares off into the side distance, bracing herself on the radio table. Her free hand mimics the one bracing her body, in a stylized, artificial pose. Her fresh-faced demeanour contrasts with Robert's more worldly and serious expression. And what do their figures encircle? Here is a parlour radio with an elephant atop it. Was this a treasured object? Is there symbolic value in an elephant appearing in a Canadian wedding photograph?

To view it today is to note the number of discordant features in this photograph: the age difference, the sober clerical garb contrasted with Florence's youthful diaphanous dress, the gazes in two different directions, as if they were distracted by too much activity in the room, although there was almost no one else there. And, most hauntingly, one is struck by the contrasting power of the two figures: Robert, occupying a good portion of the picture with his legs thrust into the centre, while Florence is crowded into the margin, as if she were awaiting his bidding. And very likely, he did give her directions of how the photograph should

Florence standing on the log manse stoop, Cartier, 1939.

appear to others. Only when viewing a photograph like this in retrospect does one notice that the figures are presented as unequal in power.

In the above photograph, Florence stands on the stoop of the log manse in Cartier soon after her marriage to Robert in 1938. Wearing a light feminine dress with short sleeves on a day when snow remained on the surface of the stoop, Florence's photograph reminds us of what an attractive young woman she was at that time. Why is she wearing such light clothing on what must have been a cold day? Does this suggest that she had few clothing choices and that she had opted for her most

Bill Fraser, Robert Killins, and George Fraser, 1939.

fashionable outfit for the photograph? Who took the picture? Was it Robert, who was still besotted by her beauty? If so, it appears that the romance continued. Florence stands hugging a post that seems to have lost the roof it supported. She is both more coquettish and relaxed than in her wedding photograph.

In this period as well, Robert came to know his two brothers-in-law, George and Bill, better. They visited periodically, and on at least one of these visits someone snapped the above photograph of Robert with Bill and George. The two young men frame Robert with his shotgun held proudly in the air. Both Robert and George sport Stetsons and bandanas around their necks as if they are playing at being cowboys. Bill grins into the camera lens, without the cowboy outfit, but clearly enjoying himself. This display of hyper-masculinity would not have been out of place in this period, except for the costumery. But it would later provide a chilling reminder of how fascinated Robert had been for decades with guns and paraphernalia surrounding firearms.

While Robert was establishing a marriage and continuing to argue with his church and presbytery councils, Gladys was having a banner decade. She was investing increasing amounts of time in her own art, taking art courses and studying with both Frank (later, Franz) Johnston of the Group of Seven and Carl Schaefer in Toronto, mainly at what is now OCAD University. The first signed painting in her oeuvre was dated 1934. By 1938, she began showing her art with the Canadian Society of Painters in Water Colour, which formally elected her to membership that year. The same year also saw a major show of her work at the Art Gallery of Toronto, now the Art Gallery of Ontario. Two of her paintings were chosen as part of the Canadian collection for display at the New York World's Fair in 1939, which she attended.

The occasion of having her paintings shown at the World's Fair must have been both exciting and validating. She briefly considered moving to New York to work on her art in a more cosmopolitan setting. She discussed this possibility with Carl Schaefer, who had become a mentor to her by 1939. He counselled against it, and she accepted his opinion. After all, she was receiving ever more recognition in Canada. It began to look to her as if she might be able to leave behind the hated teaching and earn her living through art. But progress was slow and supplies expensive on a teacher's slender salary.

Gladys's work was deeply marked by her mentors' styles from the Canadian Impressionist movement. Despite the fact that most of their work was in oil while Gladys developed as a watercolourist, many of the scenes she chose were reminiscent of the Group of Seven's subjects. One can see the influence of Johnston in her preferred colour palette of golds, oranges, greens, blues, and ochres (see especially Johnston's *The Dark Woods*, 1921). There are echoes as well of A.Y. Jackson's works with the rolling hills and trees of Georgian Bay, and of J.E.H. MacDonald's *The Solemn Land* from 1921.

Gladys came to prefer landscapes and still lifes to most other subjects in her art, but she also often chose derelict buildings set in rural landscapes. Her penchant for rural pastoral scenes reflects the view developed by the Group of Seven that real art should profile Canadian nature, rather than humans and structures. Those old buildings also must have struck a chord in a young woman who had seen her share of rundown farms that her father had hoped to improve.

As her craft developed, Gladys's paintings became darker, certainly darker than either Franz Johnston's or A.Y. Jackson's work on which she had earlier modelled her own work. She loved stormy skies, and many of her paintings feature layered clouds in greys and blues. The skies are reminiscent of Carl Schaeffer's in, for example, his *Storm on the Horizon*. Most of Gladys's canvases that survive had been doubled, with a painting on both sides. This spoke to her poverty and her uncertainty about the quality of her work. Unlike the members of the Group of Seven, Gladys was a solitary artist, labouring in relative obscurity. One is reminded of Emily Carr in enumerating the many challenges she faced to do her art at all.

Robert continued to struggle with his clerical appointments but certainly not publicly (his family knew nothing of the difficulties), Gladys built her artistic reputation as a watercolourist, and Harold, the youngest sibling, was working away on his B.S.A. degree at the Ontario Agricultural College. Judging from the bundles of photographs he took of virtually every aspect of college life, the friends he made, and the studies he worked hard at, his university career was a resounding success. Always optimistic and diligent, he accepted his mother's view that he needed to work harder than others to achieve success. He became a model student, reaching the top of his class from his first year. He gloried in the course work and committed much of the lecture material to memory, being able to recount favourite lectures decades afterward. A rather extensive biography appeared for every student in his first year of university. Here was his:

Harold from the place of "rushing waters," hotels and power houses [Niagara Falls], being an enthusiastic horticulturist he has spent much of his time on fruit farms. Once he tried mixed farming, but the tragic result made him a decided specialist. During the summer of 1931 he worked at

Harold Killins in his university graduation photograph, 1936.

the Vineland Experimental Station; there he was able to study the many phases of fruit-farming and "peach culture." Harold has travelled much and is an interesting conversationalist, always eager for a discussion or argument on almost any subject. He is a conscientious student, a systematic worker and a veritable book-worm. It is Harold's intention to take the Intermediate Year, and then enter the "hort" [horticultural] option, to make a more thorough investigation of the mysteries that surround the delicious peach.

In the end, Harold chose to study bee culture for his honours essay, rather than peach culture as described here, but he never lost his love of both farming and orchard production. To everyone's surprise, including his own, he had become a top student and an authority on horticultural matters. He still couldn't spell, but that proved to be far less important than anyone had anticipated.

Harold graduated with his B.S.A. in 1936. Was there a celebration for Harold in his hour of glory? Of course not: his mother, Rachel, disparaged the degree as "farm work," unworthy of a university education. As usual, his father remained silent in the face of Rachel's withering criticism. Harold's response was to carry on by shouldering all of the work on this busy farm, not complaining that he would never be the family hero, the role that Robert had captured and would maintain no matter what his life experience. What is more, Harold never acknowledged that while his brother had taken two tries for his degree, he had managed to complete his — with an honours standing — in one, and with no drama to boot. Harold had taken longer than the allotted four years for his degree, possibly to earn money for his expenses. When asked how he felt about his achievements being ignored, he responded — ever graciously — that he knew what he had achieved, and that that was enough for him.

Even with his academic achievements, the life Harold had chosen — or that had been chosen for him as the only remaining child at home — was a stressful one. Even though there was large-scale unemployment, he had great difficulty in finding hired help for the farm. The result was that he worked from dawn to dusk every day of the week, trying to keep ahead of the avalanche of tasks. In addition, he extended his father's small apiary and sold honey on weekends at the market to make ends meet.

Eventually this lifestyle caught up with him, along with the sadness of his mother's death in 1939 from diabetes, and he was hospitalized for nervous exhaustion. He was diagnosed with depression and medicated so thoroughly that when he was discharged, he refused to take any medication ever again. And with more help and a change of profession on the horizon, he recovered and never experienced the corrosive effects of

Ethel Fry as a registered nurse before her marriage, 1936.

depression again. His hospitalization had one very positive effect, however. On hearing that her former beau was ill, Ethel Fry arranged to visit him with his old friend and her brother, Samuel Fry.

It took very little time for Ethel to realize that this short man had a big personality and heart, along with much potential. She realized her error in having ended their relationship a decade earlier. They began dating again and within months were engaged. They married in January 1940, with Harold marvelling then and over the years that such a beautiful and intelligent woman would have him. Theirs was a lifelong romance, with Harold exclaiming on cue that he had bruises all over his body from pinching himself for his great luck in having found Ethel yet again. For

Ethel and Harold on their wedding day in January 1940.

her part, Ethel resigned herself to wearing flat shoes for the rest of her long life.

As the 1930s closed, Robert's career was in a downward slide, but his marriage to Florence seemed happy for the moment. Her parents continued their war of words, as they would for many more years. Gladys's reputation as a watercolourist was on the rise, and she was excited and hopeful for a future without the demands and aggravations of teaching. Harold had taken over the family farm, married, and was providing a soft retirement for his father. But this was still the honeymoon for Robert. Hard times were about to arrive.

CHAPTER 4

Reality Strikes: 1940–1956

———————

Postwar Canada experienced nearly continuous prosperity, high employment, and the extension of the welfare state. The end of the Second World War saw hundreds of thousands of veterans returning to their communities. Canada grieved its forty-five thousand dead, but it was affluent from the war, especially in comparison to worn-out Britain and bombed-out Western Europe.

The booming domestic economy opened opportunities for everyone, and Florence and her brothers as well as Harold and Gladys would have been carried along on this tide of hopefulness as people were intent on re-working their lives after the six years of war. Robert, however, was rapidly retreating into an anti-social bubble where the wealth and optimism of the age would have had very little impact on him. And soon things were destined to become much worse.

The 1950s was a period of anti-communism in Canada, fanned by the flames of the Cold War. Robert, Gladys, and Harold all had a long history of admiring communism, especially as it was thought to have improved the lot of the Chinese from 1949 and Russia before 1953. The repression and famines in both China and Russia in this period were poorly understood in the West. Harold and Gladys held to these views more quietly, but Robert was positively and noisily supportive of communism. This was a period when most Canadians thought of that ideology as dangerous, both abroad and at home.

Socially, the 1950s was a conservative era as Canada re-established a consumer society after the demands of the war. Despite ever-increasing female labour force participation — by 1961, it stood at 22 percent[1] — the mantra of the age was that women belonged in the home, serving the needs of their families. The primacy of the nuclear family was everywhere evident, including in Robert and Florence's case.

Robert

As the 1940s dawned, Robert's arguments with the United Church councils worsened. Robert served in two parishes in the early 1940s: Depot Harbour, Ontario, and Clanwilliam, Manitoba. In these last two of his postings, he replayed the same grievances and engaged in similar tussels with the councils as in his first two parishes: he was being underpaid and overworked; his spiritual-support duties were overwhelming as parishioners expected too much from him. The congregation seemed not to appreciate his sermons, or even to understand them. It was all too much.

The difference between his first two parishes in the 1930s and these at the end of his ministry was that now he had a wife, a very young wife with no experience as a minister's partner. Florence also likely found the parish duties demanding and confusing, considering Robert's inability to translate these effectively for her. Still, given her background and inclinations, she likely would and could have been a successful minister's wife if she had been given a chance.

The records from this period suggest that Robert was probably depressed, as he had been at university. His continued inability to summon the energy to write his weekly sermons, much less contribute in any other way to the parish, added to the stress of trying to establish a marital relationship likely weighed heavily on him. Sadly, all of these factors

A visibly pregnant Florence harvests apples at her brother-in-law's farm in 1943.

contributed to the unravelling of Robert and Florence's relationship. There were likely continual arguments between them about starting a family. Parish work was divisive, too, and Robert negotiated a move to the Clanwilliam congregation, with the hope of a new start.

By 1943, Florence was at last pregnant after almost five years of unsettled marriage. She had left Robert on several occasions, frightened by his insistence that he control every aspect of her life and by his violent temper. But she always returned, or was brought back by him, a pattern

later repeated with his daughter and in situations with many other battered women and their threatening partners. How would a young woman
with few marketable skills, little confidence, and having made a presumably ideal marriage to the local minister survive on her own? Now she
was due to have a baby, and the chance of her remaking a life without
Robert was even less.

In February 1944, Florence delivered a beautiful baby girl, Pearl
Irene. The baby was named after her maternal grandmother. Her birth
made Florence inexpressibly happy, since she loved children, and was
passionate about this new baby. Happily engaged with the many demands of motherhood, Florence must have hoped that a new start was
being made in their marriage as well. Robert remained largely silent on
the baby's arrival.

By the fall of 1945, barely two years after his hopeful rebuilding of
his life and career in his last charge, Robert and Florence were gone from
Clanwilliam. From this latest parish as well, there was no testimonial
dinner to bid them goodbye, no comments in the annual report, no sign
of a parting gift offered by the congregation. At Clanwilliam, Robert
had clashed repeatedly with the church council. Long afterward, one of
the Clanwilliam parishioners, Marshall Cook, described the regular dis-
agreements between the church officials and their uncooperative minister. "He would never stick to the rules," said Cook. "He was always a law
unto himself. He ran everything his own way." On his love of guns, Cook
noted that "he loved shooting and he was forever getting into trouble for
shooting game out of season. He was not too bad a preacher but he was
an odd fellow."[2]

Robert had made himself so scarce in the parish that most people
might not have noticed he was gone. Cook noted, "He went away very
quietly and no one ever heard from him again. He didn't even know
where he was going to."

This time, the break with the United Church was complete. Robert
did not bother to submit his resignation to the placement committee for
a full year, possibly because he remained hopeful that he might request
yet another parish and that, with the right one, he might yet thrive.

The land around Ruskin was densely wooded.

When Robert got around to formally resigning from his posting in the fall of 1946, he was living with Florence in Ruskin, British Columbia, a small settlement, about thirty-five kilometres east of Vancouver, on the north shore of the Fraser River. Located close to the community of Mission, Ruskin was a dusty mill village with logging operations feeding the sawmill, a scattering of houses, a dairy, and some vegetable farms.

The dense forest was traversed only by logging roads, as seen in the photograph above. With so many loggers without accommodation, Robert decided to build one-room shacks on land he had bought and resell them to the local workers. The photograph shows the rugged conditions of the area as well as the isolation. Robert had inherited a bit of money from his parents, giving him the capital needed to begin his enterprise. However, before he could begin to build a shack, he needed to clear the land in true pioneer style. He must have hearkened back to the days of his parents when they were homesteading in Alberta. But his parents did not face the task of clearing scrub brush and forest before putting up a house. How did the family survive before he cleared the land and then

Robert, Pearl, and Florence in front of one of the larger shacks he built for his family in Ruskin in 1946.

built his first shack? It could not have been easy. And the already tattered marriage would not have been helped by the privation they experienced in those early months, along with the rain and the mud.

Why had Robert chosen this retreat from the shambles of his career? It is possible that he had read about Ruskin, named after the British utopian socialist and essayist, because a number of the town leaders were devotees. Although no utopian community ever took hold there, it did become fertile ground for the Canadian cooperative movement, especially in the sawmill. He might well have been drawn west to live in a cooperative community, if only on the fringes, since he had long supported the movement. Importantly, too, he was drawn back to the wilderness.

Maybe Robert thought of the move as bringing him back to the land and making some money in this last bid to reconcile with Florence. Perhaps they could start over in this little idealistically founded town

The local postmaster, Pearl with her doll, Florence, and Robert stand outside their shack in Ruskin, British Columbia, in 1946.

without the challenges of leading a parish where the congregants had not warmed to Robert. Robert would build a series of shacks here. He learned to do this efficiently with so little wastage that he "could put into his pocket the leftovers and walk away" as he told Brian years later. In one instance, he built and sold a shack for about six hundred dollars in nearby Mission. It was one of many, and he did make money from this venture.

Much of the rest of Robert's time was taken up with building a shack for Florence, Pearl, and himself. They had not brought a lot with them from Clanwilliam, in addition to an old wringer-washer machine among their provisions. However, indispensable items that he would not leave behind were his guns and ammunition.

Robert and Florence's shack, shown in the above photographs, was built of rough timber. One wonders why the only surviving photograph from this period includes the couple and the local postmaster. They were indeed isolated, and so the periodic visit of one of the only officials around was likely a highlight to be recorded.

One evening, a fire broke out in the clapboard house. The fire department was summoned but refused to come even close to the house, much less save any articles, because Robert's stash of guns and ammunition was exploding along with the house's dry siding. This was the first time that his collection of guns became public knowledge. From here forward, he would never be without firearms: a sawed-off shotgun, handguns, and a great deal of ammunition. Robert, Florence with the baby, and the local firefighters each stationed themselves behind protective trees, shouting to one another as the fire ignited another volley of shots. "Is there more ammunition?" they shouted to Robert. "Oh yes, lots more," he assured them. The firefighters watched from afar with Florence and Robert until the shack burnt to the ground with nothing saved.

Within days, Florence had left with her toddler, leaving behind the ashes of her house and her marriage. There had been too many fights, too much failure, too many promises broken. She deserved better, and the fire had burned away all of the remaining illusions. She took only what she could pull from the smouldering ruins and carry, and then fled.

Robert remained. Angry, tired, he had lost everything. With smoke in his hair and eyes, he brooded as he poked through the embers looking for anything that survived the blaze. His anger grew as he wrestled with the litany of failures in his life. At the age of thirty-nine, he had been left with nothing. As he had done in the past, he blamed those who had failed him: the United Church of Canada officials, Florence, Florence's family, even the fire fighters who refused to extinguish the flames.

Florence and Pearl

We will never know how Florence managed to get herself and her toddler across Canada after their shack burned to the ground. She would have had no clothing or supplies for herself or her child, no food, and no money to purchase what she needed. But Florence had shown her mettle earlier when her own family experienced hunger and unrelenting poverty. She was a first-class problem-solver then, and she took this crisis in her marriage and financial situation in stride now. At least she had escaped Robert, she thought.

She might have had free rail service because of her father's job on the CPR, but that would not have covered any of her other immediate needs, or Pearl's either. For example, did she stop with her family in Winnipeg? There is no evidence of this. She knew that her parents were unsympathetic to her ending her marriage with Robert. Despite Pearl Viola and Ira not having any affection for Robert, in their opinion Florence was bound to continue in an unhappy marriage, just as they had managed to do in theirs. She and countless other Canadians, trapped in unions that were potentially dangerous and certainly miserable for all concerned, were expected to simply carry on and make the best of a bad union.

Did Florence have any other relatives to support her? While her brother George was always ready to help, he was in no position to provide for her and Pearl, and she would not have imposed on him to do so. He was newly married himself, and working long hours. Her brother Bill was still living with his parents.

Gladys

During this difficult period, Gladys's role was pivotal in Florence's support network, both in her initial escape from Robert and through the succeeding years. In her own crusty way, Gladys would have raised Florence's confidence by her matter-of-fact pushing back against Robert's most outrageous assertions and actions. Along with her parents and younger brother, Gladys apparently held Robert in awe for his presumed academic and career achievements. But as a hard-nosed art teacher and artist, and six years his senior, she was a perceptive audience for Robert's many excuses for his failures. As well, she was not blind to some of his personality problems. As Robert's crises mounted, she inserted herself into Florence and Robert's lives and tried to help. Might Florence with Pearl in tow have stopped in Parry Sound to visit with Gladys and get her bearings on that first wild flight across the country? This seems very likely.

Gladys and Florence had always respected each other, and as the years advanced, they forged a bond. Aside from occasional visits, this was mainly through letters. When Robert and Florence took the United Church posting in Depot Harbour in 1944, for example, Gladys bought a small cottage relatively close by in Parry Sound to be able to visit them. During the brief sojourn in Ruskin, British Columbia, Gladys travelled west from her home in Orangeville, Ontario, to lend a hand, although she seems to have ended her stay before the shack burned. No other family but Gladys is known to have visited them in Ruskin, where Robert and Florence were in full retreat from society. Letters were exchanged between the two women, and Gladys later gifted Florence with several paintings.

Despite being opposite in personality from Florence, in that she had more maturity, education, and professional standing as a teacher and artist to refine her public image, Gladys provided clandestine support for her, particularly during periods when she feared for her life. While Gladys would not have been able to identify with Florence's strong maternalism, she could empathize with Florence's fears. The fact that Gladys could not change Robert's obsessions, his anti-social personality, and fury over so many issues does not mean that she did not try to find solutions for these deep-seated problems. Her attempts to do so might well have been the subject matter of their protracted and angry verbal duels, which were observed by many.

By 1946, when Florence likely spent time with her on her journey across Canada, Gladys was financially and psychologically able to lend support. At that time, Gladys's artistic career was thriving. She was in the full flower of her most productive and recognized period as an artist. By the late 1940s, it appeared that she might be able to make a living as an independent watercolourist. Exhibitions were held at the Niagara Falls Public Library in 1948, at the Art Gallery of Toronto in 1951, and at the Gallery of Fine Arts in Owen Sound in 1954, where she had thirty paintings on display.

Hopeful for her future, Gladys quit her hated teaching position in 1947. She knew she would have to live on a small income from her pension after only twenty-three years of service, but she was confident that by selling even a few canvases each year, she could live comfortably. However life was hard for Gladys as a struggling artist. By the mid-1940s, she herself was in her forties and increasingly eccentric without the stabilizing force of having to appear before students on a daily basis. Gladys had never made much money through her art, and her small pension did not go far in this period before teachers' unions were able to command better salaries and pensions for their retired members. There was little money to purchase new clothing or even nutritious food. The Blue Mikado tea set lay forgotten. To whom would she serve tea now?

Still, Gladys experimented with novel techniques in this period. When her coloured paintings are viewed in black-and-white tones, her shading is more obvious, which adds depth to the scenes. The use of dark on light tones emphasize the lighter areas in her paintings. Gladys used both "wet on wet" and "wet on dry" techniques to create impressionistic effects,[3] also reminiscent of the Group of Seven.[4]

Accounts of Gladys at this time describe a woman who had almost completely jettisoned feminine qualities. Her outfits were comprised of lumberjack flannel shirts with men's pants and rough boots; her hair was short and askew; and she chain-smoked, so her hands were rough and stained. She rolled her own cigarettes using strong tobacco. Aside from the cigarettes, her uniform was much like Robert's, and certainly their personalities had converged in many ways. She rarely invited guests into her primitive cottages, but when she did the cooking, she was distracted and basic. Stories abound of barely edible meals, only partly cooked. The delicate tea set was no longer on display but lay bundled up to be given away.

Her especially fractious relationships with men by the 1940s were striking to her family. Her only friends by this time were women, and even in these relationships she was regarded as a difficult person. Her temper was often on display. She seemed unable to discuss or debate an issue quietly. Any topic broached resulted in a shouting match with her interlocutor, where only one of the pair could win. Most of her visitors were so alarmed at her heightened emotions on everyday topics that they retreated into silence, allowing her to "win" the discussion. Only one person refused to be shouted down, and that was Robert, who himself brayed at anyone brave enough to discuss issues with him.

Brother and sister were well matched: neither of them would allow anyone else time to state their opinion on a matter, nor did they believe that anyone else had ideas that should be considered. One member of the family recalls Robert and Gladys standing on opposite sides of a building lot screaming at each other. These remarkable demonstrations of distanced shouting matches and stubbornness were not staged to entertain others: each genuinely believed that they had to win the verbal battles, and so they carried on and on. Win or lose, someone would eventually storm away, muttering to themselves, shouting over their shoulder, heading back to their isolated cottage, to rehash the abuse and wait for the next battle in which to twist the blade. They became stranger and more frightening to those outside their closed circle. These yelling matches carried on for long periods, suggesting that the issues being discussed were not easily resolved. Is it possible that Gladys was engaging Robert head-on as his life spiralled out of control?

Even in Gladys and Robert's shared cynicism and screaming matches, Gladys was far less troubled than Robert in this or any other period. She continued to paint. She had always loved dogs and cared for one after another almost maternally. She was also capable of flashes of kindness as she tried to take on the role of a supportive aunt. In the early 1950s, she invited two of her nephews to stay with her for a month at her cottage in the Hockley Valley. As they recalled this awkward visit during which she expected the eight- and ten-year-olds to occupy their own time, they suffered from her sharp tongue and violent temper, which erupted regularly through clouds of cigarette smoke. Had she forgotten that she did not like children? Finally, after some long-forgotten rule had been broken, she called her brother Harold to come and pick up his children. She packed up both boys and left them standing alone on the shoulder of the highway, waiting for their father to make the four-hour drive to collect them. When asked for an assessment, almost seventy years later, one of the boys offered, "completely terrifying."

Gladys, dressed up and sitting on the stoop of her cabin, in the 1940s.

Ill health dogged Gladys, and she talked about neighbours spying on her or plotting accidents. She was suspicious about gallery owners' motives in showing her work, and refused to allow her paintings to be shown for sale after 1955. Her acrimony stands opposed to evidence that at least a few gallery owners admired her work and tried to convince her to place paintings with them. Gladys was chronically low on confidence about the quality of her work, leaving many paintings unfinished. She was increasingly distrustful of anyone invading her space. By 1956, when she moved to Dun Church, near Parry Sound, her painting output was much reduced, although she did continue to paint. Even the paint and watercolour paper were rationed and of relatively lesser quality. She is estimated to have produced hundreds of paintings in all, with an unknown quantity sold in her lifetime.

Harold

In the early 1940s, Harold and his new bride, Ethel, continued to care for Robert John on the farm in Fonthill. Hiring help when he could, Harold struggled to maintain the farm during the Second World War and afterward. Life on the farm was dominated by the thriving beekeeping business, with ready markets for the honey in Hamilton and Welland. Harold continued to get up at 2:00 a.m. on Saturdays to prepare for his weekly trip to sell honey at the Welland Market. He replanted the pear orchard and vineyard as well as a huge asparagus patch. Prices were generally high for farm products, but labour continued in short supply. The worry of weather and price changes ate away at Harold and sapped his enthusiasm for farming.

His family was growing, too: a son, Wesley, was born in 1941, another son, David, in 1944, and a daughter, Sharon, in 1947. After Robert John died in 1942, Harold and Ethel continued to work the farm. As the decade wore on, they decided that the needs of their family and Harold's mental well-being demanded a move to the city. In 1949, the family moved to Brampton, commissioning Robert to take on the construction of a house for the family. The project took a number of months with Harold and Ethel and even young Wesley helping as they could.

Robert was not inclined to like children, or even adults, whom he regarded as beneath him. In the period of building the house for his brother, however, he forged a relationship with Wesley, then about eight, which sustained them throughout their lives. Wesley patterned his friendship with Robert on his father's, who continued to admire Robert, indulging his increasingly eccentric mannerisms. During the coming difficult years for Robert, he and Wesley stayed in touch, arranging regular visits.

Meanwhile, Harold was re-establishing his own career in the feed business, working for Purity Feeds Ltd as a salesman. Long days and weeks away from his family while driving around the countryside to visit farmers meant that Harold was not available to help Robert with his domestic problems, even if he had been asked, which he was not. The marital fracture as a subject was studiously avoided in family conversations.

Florence seems to have contacted Harold and Ethel about her problems, but in any case, she would have known that Harold's sympathies would be with Robert. In fact, Harold seemed constitutionally unable to criticize Robert on almost any matter. Florence would not have expected support from him, and she seems not to have received it, either.

Florence and A.D. Hall

After leaving Robert, Florence disembarked from the train in the lovely small town of Colborne, in eastern Ontario. Colborne was settled in the late eighteenth century by late Loyalists from Virginia led by Joseph Abbott Keeler, called "Young Joe." It rapidly became the largest settlement in the Township of Cramahe. Situated about halfway between York and Kingston on the Kingston Road, in the nineteenth century Colborne became a convenient rest stop for stagecoaches. By the 1850s, it had three railway stations, serving the Grand Trunk, the Canadian Pacific, and the Canadian Northern Railways.[5] It positively boomed in the 1920s and '30s, when its convenient location made it a prime rum-running centre during Canadian and American Prohibition.

There were streams for mills and apple orchards aplenty, with mixed farming supporting local families. Locals could choose from six churches: the Roman Catholic, St. Andrews Presbyterian, the Pentecostal, Prospect Missionary Church, Baptist, Anglican, and the largest, the Methodist Church, which became the United Church in 1925. By 1946, when Florence arrived, Colborne had the status of a town with a good number of services: there were banks, hotels, various shops, a Land Registry office, law offices, a post office, insurance brokers, barber shops and hair salons, a Masonic hall, a Legion, an ice rink, an opera house, and its own power-generating station. It had grand houses and many modest ones: something for everyone.

Why was this Florence's destination? It is possible that she was headed somewhere else but became exhausted and disembarked from the train earlier than expected. Perhaps she knew someone there, although this

A.D. Hall, graduating photograph from his law studies, Osgoode Hall, 1920.

is belied by her isolation; perhaps she hoped that employment would be found in a town rather than a major city. Whatever her plans, there she met local lawyer A.D. (Austin Davis) Hall. It is possible that she originally went to him to explore how she could get a divorce from Robert. A.D. was fifty-three years old; Florence was twenty-six, but nevertheless they seemed perfectly matched.

Florence and A.D. became a couple soon after meeting, and with that her life took a decided turn for the better. A.D. wasn't wealthy, but he was an established lawyer and he could easily provide for Florence and Pearl. He was deeply respected in the town, providing a social foundation for Florence. Long separated from his wife, A.D. was widowed about the time he met Florence. He had a grown daughter and grandchildren in Alberta, with whom he was on warm terms.

Like Florence's father, A.D. Hall had served in the Great War. But aside from that fact, the two men were very different. Born in 1893 in Tara, Ontario, A.D. Hall had grown up in Saskatchewan. Like his brothers, he was bound to be a lawyer. One of his brothers became a judge later in life. A.D. joined the 147th Grey Overseas Battalion from Owen Sound in November 1915 while he was still a law student.

It was common during the First World War for a prominent towns-man to finance a regiment for young men in their town and surround-ing locale as a patriotic gesture. This was the source of the 147th Grey. Unfortunately, the regiment was broken up after the high casualties in-flicted on the First and Second Divisions during the Second Battle of Ypres in 1915. In that battle, chlorine gas was used for the first time, and while the First Canadian Division held on and counter-attacked the much lar-ger German divisions, the losses decimated the Canadian Corps. Further losses incurred during the 1916 battles at St. Eloi and the Somme, and the withering costs of trench warfare generally meant that subsequent battal-ions raised in Canada were broken up to reinforce the Canadian Corps.

Soldiers with a university education were often appointed from pri-vate to a non-commissioned officer. A.D. Hall was named to the position of Acting Company Quartermaster Sergeant (A/CQMS), the quarter-master of services. Hall's duties were to monitor and distribute equip-ment, ammunition, and other war material to privates. It was a good role for a lawyer. However, he wanted to directly contribute to the fighting in France rather than be left behind in England, as was the plan for his pos-ition. To become an active combatant, he relinquished his stripes and the higher salary that went with it and became a private. He was dispatched to France as part of the 4th Canadian Mounted Rifles in early November 1917, just in time for the Battle of Passchendaele.

Much has been written about the horrors of Passchendaele: General Haig's plan to regain the land around Passchendaele was regarded as both risky and foolhardy, and even unnecessary by many military authorities, including Canada's commander, Arthur Currie. This area of Flanders had been reclaimed from the sea and had poor drainage, controlled by dykes and canals. All of this was destroyed by the millions of shells fired before and during battles. The battlefield quickly turned into a swamp of mud and unburied corpses, with water-filled shell holes threatening to drown any wounded or careless soldier who strayed from the duck boards. The mud acted like quicksand, sucking its victims to their death. One soldier's anecdote described a soldier discovered up to his neck in mud. It took twenty men with ten ropes to pull him out of the mud, it was recounted. With his clothes sucked off, he stood naked and asked, "Now what about my mule I was sitting on?"

It is very unlikely that A.D. did much laughing at Passchendaele, or afterward either, considering his experience there. Regardless, he did survive the horrors of war, lending his youth and talent to the war effort. And like Ira, his personality was forged in the war years. The difference was that while Ira took to hard physical labour for the rest of his life, A.D. lent his reason and intelligence to every situation, particularly those rife with emotion. After his stint on the Western front, A.D. was posted back to England and granted a commission with the 1st Central Ontario Regiment Depot. That life was far less exciting than his service in France had been, but he also had a better chance of seeing his twenty-fifth birthday at the depot than would have been the case in France.

Upon his return from the war overseas, A.D. built a successful law practice in Colborne. It was small city concerns — wills, insurance claims, property disputes, and the like — but he forged a reputation and became a leader in the town. He joined the Masonic Order. And he was an unattached, handsome man when Florence met him.

Not long after their meeting, A.D. and Florence were living together. A.D. was a calming and fortifying presence for Florence. For the first time since her marriage to Robert, Florence did not have to worry about how she would find enough nourishing food or warm clothes. She settled easily into her new domestic life, leaving behind Robert's abuse, rants, and directives. Throughout the approximately fifteen years during which they were a couple, A.D. provided the protection and stability Florence badly needed. He was devoted to her, and she to him. With A.D., twenty-seven years her senior, Florence worried about a time when she would not have him at her side, but for the present, she lived happily with him.

A New Family

A family of their own soon arrived: in addition to Pearl, Robert's daughter, then about six, was added another daughter, Margaret, in 1950, a son, Brian, in 1952, and a third daughter, Patsy, in 1956. With Patsy's birth, Florence was still a young woman of thirty-six, now with four children.

Florence and Brian in 1953.

A.D. and Florence settled into a simple, normal life. They mainly kept to themselves, and their children report a household that was focused on the children and everyday pleasures. Stress levels were low, and laughter was common. A.D. adored the children and spent as much time with them as he could. In turn, they felt secure and loved in his presence. They called him their "Joey" as a pet name.

The children recall this period as happy and "normal." In addition to her positive outlook and sense of humour, Florence was also remembered as kind. The children recall a local homeless man calling at their door asking for food. Florence invited him inside to have dinner with the family at Thanksgiving. The man was nervous, but he agreed to sit down with them. On the table, laden with turkey and the side dishes, was a tray of Florence's hot relish to be passed around as a garnish. The tray happened to be placed by his plate, and he ate it all, to the children's astonishment. His face turned red and tears flowed down his cheeks. Somehow, he got through the meal, but he must have felt the effects of the hot relish for some time afterward.

Pearl became a good big sister to the three younger children. Pearl had the security of being a child well loved. She was treasured by both Florence and Robert in different ways and accepted by A.D. as one of the children in his care after his relationship with Florence began. The new family of Florence, A.D., and the four children lived harmoniously — except for Robert's intrusive presence.

One can see that Pearl was a loving big sister to her half-siblings in the photograph below. Here we see Pearl and Margaret sharing a moment and a chuckle. Pearl spent a great deal of time with the other children, happily helping her mother where she could. As she grew, she longed for a child of her own.

One day, several months after Florence had begun living with A.D., Robert arrived at their door. He explained that he had no intention of losing touch with his child, even if his marriage to Florence was over. He seems to have struck an arrangement with A.D. and Florence that he could regularly see Pearl. To accomplish this, Robert located himself as close as possible to wherever A.D. and Florence were living, without

Florence, Brian, Margaret, and Pearl in 1953.

actually moving into their house. Of course, this created tensions in the household as Robert visited Pearl daily, taking on supervision of her homework. Robert was vague about boundaries and regularly overstepped his position in the household, often walking into the house whenever he chose, for example. He had to be regularly reminded about the arrangement if he were to continue seeing Pearl.

A.D. had experience with mental health problems because of his marital situation. The exact nature of his wife's issues is undefined, but she may have suffered from an undiagnosed mental illness. In any case, A.D. had coped with her odd behaviour for some years when they had lived in Colborne. Eventually, she settled with her and A.D.'s daughter in

Brian and Margaret in 1954.

Alberta. She lived out her final days in long-term care. Hence, A.D. was not only patient, he was familiar with mental health crises.

Robert would disappear for significant periods when he could find a job in construction, either near home or away at relatives'. Generally, his building projects were just for himself or for Gladys, for whom he built a number of cottages. But when he was in Castleton, he kept a careful daily watch on Florence and Pearl, visiting Pearl each day. His stalking behaviour made everyone in the family nervous.

Robert replayed the script written by his mother when she had raised him: education and learning would be the most important feature of Pearl's life, just as it had been with him as a child. Robert determined that

Pearl would be brilliant, and he spent a great deal of time working with her at reading and writing, far earlier than she was ready for such skills. In later years, the daily coaching sessions turned into shouting matches with Pearl refusing to do anything asked, even when she had matured and was able to meet his expectations. Rebellion against schoolwork with Robert progressed into uprising against practising her viola or piano, or in doing simple chores. Long before she was an adolescent, Pearl had been encouraged to sharpen her skills as a rebel by watching her father's antics and by reacting against his smothering presence. Ironically, this might have been the one way in which Robert was an effective teacher.

From left: Doug (A.D.'s son-in-law), Florence, and A.D. Children from left: Dolly (partially hidden), Brian, Margaret, and Anne. (Dolly and Anne are A.D.'s granddaughters.)

Still, there were personal costs to Florence and A.D. cohabiting outside of marriage. The couple had few friends and limited contact with relatives. Robert refused to give Florence a divorce, so A.D. and Florence living together was the only possible choice. Before 1968, when divorce laws were finally relaxed in Canada, it was both an expensive and cumbersome process for marital partners to end their relationship. The children, too, suffered social ostracism as a result of this extramarital arrangement. Despite their loving home, they were "illegitimate," a term none of the children would have heard but would have been whispered in town. Margaret remembers a few school-aged "friends" in Colborne being forbidden to play with her. Shunning was a practice the children and Florence experienced early and often.

By the late 1940s, Robert had perfected his identity as an outsider, an isolate, and an eccentric in the community. He could show sympathy and lend a hand to others, particularly his siblings, but to his estranged wife and her partner he presented a severe and even menacing presence. He took to uncontrolled swearing, bellowing his orders or comments; he seemed to have no "filters." Neighbours recount that Robert often carried a Bible around with him even as he freely swore and shouted at people. He was described as seeming to have "a load on his mind. I knew he was having family trouble."[6]

The following picture shows Robert in a peaked hat and checked shirt with overalls. Those clothes comprised his "uniform," a far cry from the minister in his tidy formal suit and collar. This unvarying costume was meant to identify him as a working man, although he rarely worked at anything except building shacks. He wore this to drop off and pick up the children from school and Pearl from Sunday school. A childhood friend of Pearl's remembers his appearance in contrast to the congregation in their Sunday best.

The uniform was constant, too, because Robert rarely bathed or changed his clothes. The surviving children report that Robert was smelled before he was seen, inside the house or out: stale perspiration and dirty clothes dominate their odorous memories of him. He often chewed garlic on the assumption that it was a medicinal curative. His hands were so dirty that they appeared discoloured. The children kept a good distance from him out of wariness of becoming dirty as well, and to avoid his unprovoked pokes and slaps. Neither recalls an affectionate gesture or word from him during the ten to twelve years of their early lives. The photograph below of the threesome is representative of his affection for Pearl, on whose shoulder his hand rests, while Margaret is leaning against Pearl, not Robert, never Robert.

Robert, Pearl, and Margaret in 1952.

An example of the galoshes that Robert wore over his slippers.

Robert's diabetes was a constant source of discomfort and danger in his life. He took insulin when his condition became dire, but irregularly. In trying to cope with his diabetic thirst, he kept many bottles of water in the car, along with peppermints and large chocolate bars. The latter was not recommended for diabetics, but Robert's cravings won out. He also had major problems with his feet because of his diabetes. For some years, he had been unable to wear shoes. He wore large slippers that fit into rubber galoshes, like those pictured above.

The galoshes were held on by the metal buckles, but only a few of them were fastened in order to keep the galoshes on his feet. When he walked, the buckles jingled. The children remember hearing him before he came in sight because of the buckles clanging against one another. During his hospitalization for carbuncles and gangrene in 1962, two of his toes were amputated. The doctors recommended taking the whole foot, but he vociferously refused. The missing toes made walking that much more difficult for him.

Most neighbours were careful around Robert, giving him a wide berth whenever they encountered him. As one neighbour put it, "Castleton residents looked askance at the onetime pastor."[7] However, he was known for random acts of kindness on occasion, as well. Percy Richards, who lived about a kilometre away, described Robert as "a friendly, good neighbour. He would pick me up in town and drive me home whenever he saw me."[8]

Nevertheless, most people found him odd and frightening. He was the subject of rumours, some true, some not. A neighbour said of him, not entirely factually, that "he wore a long coat in the middle of summer, and you'd see him in bib overalls and a shirt in the middle of winter. He'd get his kids up in the middle of the night and drive off in his old car to show them Niagara Falls. He was somethin' else."[9]

Children in the area called Robert "Iron Head" behind his back, referencing Frankenstein, because of his stiff gait and the odd set of his head. His face was peculiarly expressionless, showing neither smiles nor scowls. There is no easy explanation for this rigid posture and blank facial expression, but it was notable enough in the community that when the children used the term "Iron Head" everyone knew who was being referenced.

Having a stalker living just outside one's door in a shack was unsettling to everyone, especially Florence. To escape Robert's threatening presence, the family moved suddenly and often, sometimes leaving behind their clothing and the children's toys. They moved whenever it appeared that they were in imminent danger: from Orangeville (where Gladys lived and where the two older children were born) to rural Brighton on Lake Ontario, to downtown Brighton in an apartment above a store, to Castleton on an acreage, to Colborne to the law office, and back to Castleton again. But Robert always found them, marched through the door with some excuse, and sought to re-establish his control. He would begin building a shack, and when he did so, he squatted on others' land.

The two-room law office where six people lived in fear.

The interlude when the family escaped to A.D.'s law office is notable for the privation the family was prepared to endure in order to escape Robert, and also for the warm memories the children still carry of those years when six people were crammed into two rooms. The children remember the chamber pot being located in the office's safe, the tiny kitchen where Florence struggled to make meals, and the primitive sleeping arrangements.

At the same time, living in such close quarters was pleasurable because of A.D.'s endless patience and obvious love in watching the children play. The vault held A.D.'s First World War gas mask, helmet, and sniper rifle, for example. Brian decked himself out in the full regalia regularly without any protest from A.D. The children had free rein to play with the typewriter, and, even better, the adding machine and the notary press seal. Law books made great stacking toys as the children made their own fun.

Robert would arrive regularly to get information on Pearl's locations, but he had no means of building a shack near to the law office, so the family felt relatively safe there.

In 1956, A.D. suffered a serious heart attack. Now sixty-three, he had had intimations of heart problems for some time, but this heart attack knocked him out for several weeks, and he was confined to hospital. During A.D.'s absence, Robert re-insinuated himself into the family, seeking to "help out." Life was tumultuous, with Florence worried and often absent at the hospital, her own mother caring for the children as Pearl Viola raged about Florence's lifestyle and its immorality, and with Pearl increasingly testing Robert's strict limits. A.D. had been the only person who could calm Robert and make him see that threats did his case no good. In turn, Robert seemed to respect and even fear A.D., struggling to control himself in his presence. With A.D.'s absence, and his increasing frailty once home, Robert was given more opportunity to take control of the family, and especially of Pearl.

A.D. recovered from that first heart attack, but he was a weakened man, and Robert knew it. From this point on until his death in 1962, A.D. was exhausted much of the time as he tried to maintain his law practice while the family struggled with Robert's rapidly declining health and mental balance. A.D.'s heart attack changed the dynamic of family relations, reducing A.D.'s and Florence's authority and increasing Robert's. It would be some time before the full impact of this change would be felt. And by then, it would be too late to pull Robert back from the brink.

CHAPTER 5

A Perfect Storm: 1956–1963

———

The final family crisis played out against the backdrop of postwar Canada from the mid-1950s to the early 1960s in the small hamlet of Castleton, Ontario. Castleton is situated in rolling hills about ten kilometres from Colborne, where Florence had first alighted. In the mid-1950s, Castleton had a population of about four hundred.

In the late 1940s, A.D. and Florence purchased a piece of land in Castleton. The couple dreamed of one day building a house there, but there was already an old farmhouse that was habitable. Robert seems to have built a shack on the land as his residence with A.D.'s permission. Maybe A.D. thought that if Robert were permitted to stay in Castleton, he would stop stalking the family.

In 1956, Florence and A.D. moved into the old farmhouse on the outskirts of Castleton, and A.D. began building the new home for the family. They lived intermittently between this new house and the drafty farmhouse until 1959, when Robert's stalking and strange behaviours again became so troubling that the family fled to A.D.'s law office in Colborne, where they lived in two rooms for three years.

From his arrival in Castleton in the late 1940s, Robert lived in a shack behind the old farmhouse. When the family moved there in 1956, he abandoned his old shack because it was too far away from the new house and built a new one, from which he could observe the family. Robert was used to living in shacks: he had built a series of these rough one-room buildings in Ruskin, British Columbia. He built one in Orangeville, another in Brighton, and then two more in Castleton. But in Colborne at the law office there was no room for a shack, nor would permission have been given to erect one in the town. Hence Robert was effectively shut out by the family. This accounts for their living in such cramped quarters for so long: in that setting, they were safe from him.

Robert's shack-building was classic behaviour for a stalker, and yet living in a shack outside a main residence was not unknown in that era. For example, Robert had a bachelor uncle who lived most of his life in a shack at the back of the property that had belonged to his parents and which he had inherited. The couple living in the main house rented from

An aerial photograph of Castleton in 1953.

the old man and looked out for him, especially as he aged, bringing food and medicines to him. Hence this kind of rather primitive housing was an early version of today's "granny flat" in a residence's backyard or laneway. The difference between the old uncle who lived at the back of his family's property and Robert's collection of shacks is that he squatted on other people's land. Furthermore, his presence was unwelcome to those in the main residence.

The Times They Are A-Changin'

The late 1950s and 1960s are remembered as a period of civil rights marches, protests against the war in Vietnam, free love with the invention of the birth control pill, and "Women's Lib." But none of these social changes would have affected rural Canada until at least the mid-1960s, if then. Taking second-wave feminism as a case in point, such feminist books as Simone de Beauvoir's *The Second Sex* (1953) and Betty Friedan's *The Feminine Mystique* (1963) did begin to influence how urban Canadian women understood their prescribed and restricted role in society by the late 1960s with the report of the Royal Commission on the Status of Women. But second-wave feminism did not influence rural Ontario hamlets like Castleton for decades to come.

A woman seeking relationships outside her marriage in rural settings was regarded as immoral, all conditions of her life aside. Women who acted in this way were thought to deserve physical reprimands from their husbands, and often worse than that. There was as yet no language for the abuse that such women typically endured in their homes, whether because they were seeking a new partner or just not getting a meal on the table when their husbands decreed. Indeed, we continue to see higher rates of domestic abuse in rural settings than in urban areas today. Florence was a representative victim of the systematic verbal and physical abuse meted out to her by a husband who felt that this was his right. The fact that no authorities stepped in to protect her is illustrative of the secrecy surrounding her situation, her isolation, community norms supporting any actions a man chose within his "castle" where he could do as he liked, and the absence of legislation to protect women in domestic settings.

This was also a period of secularization, with Quebecers abandoning the Roman Catholic Church during the Quiet Revolution after 1960 and English Canadians moving away from the mainline churches, just as Robert himself had done. "Campus revolts" marked post-secondary education in the 1960s. Even if these changes did not resonate in Castleton, Ontario, the culture was changing. For example, by the mid-1950s media images of sexualized young men and women, especially women, were common. Youths were shown openly smoking and drinking. Shocked observers saw instances of hedonism in newspapers and magazines, in popular books and, by the 1950s, on television. Hints in the music of the era suggested that entertainment extended to open sexual activity. And the music was loud, so loud that Robert could not bear it.

Advice literature concentrated on the problem of the "teenager," a term coined in the mid-1950s with the publication of Erik Erickson's enormously popular book, *Childhood and Society* (1950) and with the 1955 release of the movie *Rebel Without a Cause*, starring James Dean. From this cultural avalanche focusing on the sexualized teenager, apparently liberated from social norms that had applied to previous generations, parents concluded that adolescents who were seeking an identity to carry them into adulthood were prone to rebellion and vulnerable to making terrible life choices that would limit their futures. These worries were especially acute for the middle class trying to distinguish themselves from the lower orders. Poor teenagers were assumed to be especially wayward, and poor teenage boys downright dangerous.

In 1960, Pearl was sixteen years old, an age when parents of conservative leanings would have quaked for their daughter's safety. But in this climate of presumed freedom from any of the rules that had kept their parents' generation in check, and with the cultural emphasis on the dangers presented daily to teenagers, a parent like Robert would have reasonably enough been terrified and pugnacious about his daughter and her newfound interest in boys. What worried Robert most about Pearl being drawn into this culture of licence and rebellion was that it was occurring in small-town Castleton, populated by farm boys and factory workers who were, in his judgment, poorly educated and "going nowhere." Any man who might have come near Pearl would have been firmly jettisoned by Robert.

Robert held an ambivalent class position. Once he had been solidly middle class as a student and cleric. His current status, drawing on welfare and living a precarious existence financially, was not middle class. However, his hopes for Pearl were great, and his fears even stronger that she would descend into the class of those he saw around her. Robert found himself the only person who seemed concerned about all of this, as Florence worked on maintaining strong ties with Pearl to help her navigate her adolescence.

Today we are hyper-aware of the danger of guns, especially when they are in the hands of unstable people. We are treated on an almost weekly basis to horrific stories of mass murders, mainly in the republic south of us, but also occasionally in Canada. In the 1960s, people did not see mass murders depicted on TV or in newspapers, and they did not expect a mass murderer to be in their midst in a quiet small town. Although many people knew that Robert had a shotgun, and we heard from a number of respondents who as children had found themselves sitting on a shotgun hidden under a blanket in Robert's car, no one seemed to suspect that he would use it. Many people in the area hunted, so his gun toting was not seen as particularly notable. The same behaviours today would raise many warning flags. But it was a different era.

In fact, the late 1950s and early 1960s was a period when TV Westerns were all the rage. Robert's favourite program on TV was *Gunsmoke*, but had he had the opportunity to watch more TV, he would have had many other Western-inspired programs from which to choose. All of these celebrated the Western gunslinger in various forms: *Roy Rogers, The Lone Ranger, Wyatt Earp, Maverick, Have Gun, Will Travel, Wagon Train, The Rifleman, Rawhide*, and on and on. Some of these gunslingers were men of peace, some were not. All made their way in a hyper-masculine landscape through marksmanship, and all revered their guns, just as

Robert did. In being fascinated with guns and gunslingers, Robert was part of a gigantic audience celebrating gun-play and rough masculinity that we can scarcely imagine today.

The Hamlet of Castleton

Founded in the mid-nineteenth century, Castleton was the township seat. The handsome municipal hall reflected its status to the surrounding farming community. Businesses and houses were clustered around several mills, including the Purdy Mill, which still stands. One main street ran through town. The hamlet at various times could boast a grist mill, sawmill, shingle and stave mills, a cheese factory, several cottage industries (including a carpet factory), hotels, stores, five churches, a bank, an egg-grading station, a public library, and a post office. In its early years, medicine shows often visited in which a travelling troupe of entertainers staged skits and jokes to encourage townsfolk to buy patent medicines offering purported cures. Female impersonators and comedians in blackface were common in the area, as were travelling beauty contests.

The hamlet is also said to accommodate departed spirits, including a young woman named Margaret Harnden Quinn. Margaret stayed at the then called Union Hotel to receive medical treatment for advanced tuberculosis. She was due to be married, but the date needed to be moved up because she was declining quickly. Given that she was unable to stand, the wedding ceremony was arranged in her room as she lay abed. Her family did not want her to die a spinster. They took the two-piece wedding dress and managed to get the top on her. The skirt was another matter, however. It was draped across the coverlet as she lay only partly conscious under it. The wedding photographs showed her new husband holding her hand as she slept. She died in the room soon after. Many people have felt Margaret's spiritual presence and believe that she still occupies that room.[1]

Castleton had a variety of community groups. There was a Women's Institute and a United Church women's group, as well as a choir. But none of these would have welcomed Florence, even though she had been so deeply involved in church life in her youth. Her lack of grounding in the community increased her isolation.

Castleton became a distribution centre for some of the products from the surrounding farms. Mixed farming, tobacco, and especially apple crops dominated in that area in the 1950s and 1960s. The landscape was dotted with old farmhouses, like the one Florence, A.D., and the children occupied outside of Castleton, and various outbuildings, including barns. Jane Urquhart writes about a Castleton barn being moved by rollers, planks, and capstans from one family farm to another: "The number of workhorses used fluctuated between twenty and two hundred, depending on who was telling the tale." After this prodigious task, a windstorm destroyed the barn on the same night it had been moved.[2]

The Killins-Hall family lived on the borderland between the hamlet and the surrounding countryside. They had neighbours across the concession road, but also much privacy. The next chapter offers a map of Castleton and the Killins compound, which eventually grew to two houses and two shacks.

The land surrounding the farmhouse was grassland with hedges here and there. There were gullies cutting the land in several places, making it necessary to walk around these to get to the far-flung neighbours. The land next to theirs had at one time been cultivated, and barbed wire still separated that tract from A.D. and Florence's property.

The Advancing Storm

In the seven years before the murders, several factors slowed the advancing storm, while at least three developments sped up the disintegration of the family dynamic. Holding back the disaster was A.D.'s continued mediation of situations that could easily have developed into gun battles or worse and Margaret's developing role as a kind of mediator-in-training. Of the factors that exacerbated Robert's furies, most important was his own declining health. Adding to the speed with which the situation disintegrated was Florence's growing confidence and assertiveness, Pearl's adolescent rebellion, and A.D.'s death.

Margaret, Florence and A.D.'s oldest child, became central between 1955, when she was still a small child, and 1963. At first unconsciously, she was the nexus of much of the action before and during the familicide. Chosen by her mother as a confidante and intermediary in many of the crises leading to the murders, Margaret witnessed all of the major events that led directly to the tragedy, offering a quiet presence. This should not be surprising: possessed of a calming nature very like A.D. Hall's, Margaret was outside the troubled circle of Florence/Pearl/Robert. She could, and did, support her mother by unquestioningly doing as directed; she acted as a liaison between Florence and Pearl, especially after the latter married; she was also a liaison between Florence and Gladys in the final days; she presented no threat to Robert and even offered a measure of companionship as Robert hurtled toward disaster.

With Margaret often came her younger brother, Brian, who in turn was quiet, equally as observant, and a typical, active, and clever little boy. Between them, they worked as a kind of tag team, witnessing and processing troubling incidents, providing information to Florence and Pearl, and protecting each other from the worst of Robert's furies. Both survived the firestorm because of their pluck and strategic knowledge, gained from years of circling warily around fighting parties. Without their collective memories, grounded in a pattern of family discord, we would have little idea of what gave rise to the final calamity. Without Margaret's mediation, both conscious and instinctive, of circumstances far beyond her control, the situation would have degenerated earlier than it did. At the time of the murders, Margaret was twelve.

Gladys

As the storm gathered in Castleton, Gladys was facing ill health and depression; she had all but stopped painting, having lost confidence in

Gladys building an outhouse for one of her cabins with Pearl in the late 1940s.

both her artistic talent and in her ability to sell her work. She was also poor, subsisting on her small teachers' pension.

To make ends meet, Gladys became preoccupied with money-making schemes, just as her father had done earlier and as Robert continued doing as well. Through the late 1940s and '50s, she had Robert build cottages for her that she then hoped to rent out to tourists. She also helped with construction projects herself, as is evident in the above photograph.

In the voting records for 1957 and 1958, she is listed as a "Tourist Operator." But the cabins were in out-of-the-way places that did not excite much public interest. This venture seems to have had limited success, and by the early 1960s, she had abandoned this plan also. Meanwhile, it put her in close proximity to her brother, and the arguments between them were legion. Margaret recalls:

> On several occasions my brother and I visited Gladys at her shack in the Hockley Valley; even as children we knew that this small wiry woman was a force to be reckoned with. Her voice was high and piercing, and her manner abrupt and gruff. She and her brother Robert regularly engaged in screaming matches that I can only deduce were about money and/or lifestyle. Neither ever conceded the match. I can still clearly visualize us as children sitting high on the nearby rock clusters watching this confusing battle of words.
>
> However, during the calm interludes, the teacher in Gladys would "kick in" and she would supply us with paints, brushes, glue, and paper. And there was also instruction! We learned how to make paper puppets as well as papier mâché figure heads using a water and flour mixture applied over old light bulbs. We loved this creativity but we were always cautious in trying to avoid doing something "ignorant." One time I was unlucky enough to burn my fingers on Gladys's permanently hot wood stove, and Gladys made a paste of water and baking soda to soothe my fingers. To this day I clearly remember the tongue-lashing I got when I accidentally put my fingers into the papier mâché paste instead of the baking soda paste.
>
> When we were left alone, which happened often, we were not afraid to explore the inside and outside of Gladys's shack. Without question, we were told not to touch or break anything, but that didn't always deter us. Gladys's shack smelled of cigarette smoke, burnt food, and dog. Her belongings were few, but she had books, paints, tools, and all things necessary to roll your own cigarettes. I remember

Gladys's cigarette dish.

the books: a handful of art books plus a book about the lost island of Atlantis, my favourite. We would look in these books and touch just about everything else. In later years, I was given one of her still life paintings in which she has staged one of her art books. The only attractive objects that I remember seeing were the small porcelain cigarette dishes with lids. One of these dishes to this day still has the stains of tobacco.

Robert's Mental and Physical Decline

Throughout this period, Robert's behaviour was increasingly worrisome to everyone who interacted with him. He presented as confused and sleepy at times, but he could easily become overexcited, shouting, swearing, and striking out at whoever was within range. He was stubborn beyond reason, taking to a notion and refusing to change his mind in the face of evidence to the contrary. He was paranoid about innocent factors and unconcerned when real danger presented itself. He had increasing difficulty hanging on to a consistent line of argument, resorting to shouting and even poking or slapping when his ability to argue effectively deserted him. He slept badly and was probably malnourished from his diet of canned goods.

At the same time, Robert possessed a kind of dark charisma for many people that is difficult to credit in hindsight. He had always been intelligent, and he was still, although with the worrisome additional features of a hair-trigger temper and irrationality. He impressed many people with his education and "book smarts," particularly those who did not see themselves as measuring up to his intelligence. To the end, he displayed confidence in his own assessments of people and trumpeted his small victories over those who seemed intent on making his life difficult. This magnetism worked in Robert's favour as people tried to placate him and deferred to what they took to be his superior reasoning powers. How else can we explain the family's tolerance in allowing him to live in a shack outside their back door? How else can we credit the imaginative stories that circulated about him in the community, where he was both feared and seemingly admired?

Robert's mistrust and hatred of doctors, "quacks," and hospitals resulted in more serious health problems than deep fatigue and malnutrition. In the late 1950s, he developed large carbuncles on his neck and leg. He would come into the family's living room from his shack and order Florence to clean and dress his weeping abscesses. To the children, the appearance of the lesions was horrifying enough but far worse was the foul smell that emanated from them. Even though Florence and A.D. insisted that Robert go to the hospital, he adamantly refused and moved himself into the woodshed attached to the main house when he could no longer stand. Only after he slipped into a coma did Florence feel secure enough to call an ambulance. She was told that he was near death and most likely wouldn't survive.

Florence herself collapsed from exhaustion and was admitted to hospital at the same time as Robert and was placed in the same ward.

While there, she could clearly hear his shouting and cursing. She begged the staff not to tell Robert that she was on the same floor. Meanwhile, Florence's parents had travelled from British Columbia to help care for the four children. During their visit, Ira demonstrated kindness to the children in a way that Pearl Viola could not. He made a garden with Brian and comforted the children. Fully expecting Robert to die, they burned the stained bedding, clothes, papers, books, and furniture from Robert's shack in a huge bonfire. Over the years, Robert had made it abundantly clear that he loathed Florence's parents, often calling them "ignorant and useless." Her parents were so afraid of Robert that they fled back to Vancouver when they heard he was leaving the hospital and returning home. Florence returned home to a house in chaos, children who had come down with the flu, and a furious and wrathful Robert.

Robert was permanently maniacally furious from this point on, blaming and threatening all who came near him. He had become an even angrier man: angry that he had developed diabetes (a dreaded disease that had killed his mother), angry that he had had two toes amputated as a consequence of a gangrene infection, angry that he was now forced to inject himself with insulin, angry that he was left with painful feet resulting from diabetic nerve damage, and angry at the "quacks" who suggested he should have his foot amputated. He refused the foot amputation, but for the first time in his life he begrudgingly took a doctor's advice about continuing the insulin injections, which undoubtedly saved his life.

His appearance was careless, and his behaviour increasingly eccentric. Because of his painful feet, he took to wearing slippers inside loose rubber galoshes, which he left unbuckled. He never again wore shoes. The family's only protection was to stay out of his way and move again.

Extended family continued to notice Robert acting strangely. In 1961, Robert, Margaret, and Brian attended his nephew Wesley's wedding in London, Ontario. Robert and the children arrived in his rattletrap car, piled high with blankets that hid firearms on the seats. The car was packed with quart jars of drinking water and bag after bag of peppermint candies to address his diabetic system. They were late, they reported, because Robert had been pulled over by the police. He only drove at night.

He was driving erratically, as was common with him, and the policeman thought he was drunk. He checked Robert's drinking mug and found only strong coffee (which he boiled, in bush fashion) with a sludge of sugar. The policeman issued a warning, and Robert settled down for a nap with the children keeping watch for any other authorities.

At the wedding, Robert talked loudly and gestured wildly. The family noticed that Robert walked rigidly. He looked dishevelled in one of his old, out-of-fashion clerical suits. Whispers circulated about what might be ailing Robert to cause him to act this way. The children recall being very uncomfortable and embarrassed because of the whispering, but Robert noticed nothing. The children worried that the whispering was about them.

On another occasion, Robert conscripted Margaret and Brian into service as he dug a well. Robert had used a dowser or a divining rod to locate the water, and he was convinced that he would have a fine well once the water source had been found. He dug all day, becoming increasingly frustrated at finding only dry ground. Margaret and Brian were first stationed at the top, delegated to winch up the pails of dirt, dump them and send them back down the deep twelve-foot hole. When the hole became too narrow, Brian was sent down to continue the digging. His feet were wet from the water seeping. The task went on and on, with no stopping for meals or bathroom breaks. In desperation, and so terrified of Robert that she said nothing about her distress, Margaret soiled her pants. She carried on working, too afraid to ask for a rest, as Robert railed at the task at hand. Working long after bedtime, in very cold temperatures, now with Brian's feet soaked, Margaret and Brian went without food; they never complained.

On several other occasions, Robert invited Brian and Margaret to accompany him into the woods. There he showed the children how to fire guns using live ammunition. He referenced *Gunsmoke*, the TV program, to the children. Apparently, shooting was supposed to be fun. The children were directed to hold and aim the gun in each case. At the time, Margaret was about eight and Brian was six. Both were terrified but unable to speak their terror in case it set Robert off on another rampage. If he noticed their discomfiture, he said nothing, and perhaps would have enjoyed the fear he was engendering in the children.

Robert's imperviousness to people's views of him was not a point of pride or of embarrassment. In fact, he appeared to have no concept of how others saw him. Having been a part of the middle class, he now freely blew his nose on the ground. A minister who had delivered formal sermons on Christian principles now swore and shouted at everyone. Those around him drew the conclusion that he felt unaccountable for his actions and entitled to do whatever he chose. Or were there other factors that caused him not to notice others' reactions to him?

Margaret, with her hand on Patsy's shoulder, Pearl, and Brian in 1961.

Robert was increasingly isolated during this period, including from his own siblings, who might have urged him to reconsider his irrational position on many issues. Gladys was occupied with the struggle to make a living after she had all but given up selling her art, fighting off depression and self-recrimination in the process. After having sold the Killins family farm, Harold was building his career in animal health and nutrition. The family had relocated to Brantford in an old house that stood by the railroad tracks. He and Ethel were fully occupied in building one of the Canadian Mortgage and Housing Corporation–planned houses several streets away. The children were growing, and Ethel's father fell ill, requiring a good deal of time spent at the Fry family farm.

In 1960, Harold was transferred with his family to the Lower Mainland near Surrey, British Columbia. This took them completely away from lending a hand with Robert. Thereafter, in 1962, they were transferred again, this time to Calgary.

Photographs like the one above, showing a happy, well-dressed, and healthy family of children, were circulated to relatives and friends. But behind this cheerful middle-class exterior was a family caught in escalating anxiety and violence. The mildest trigger could set Robert off on a path of destruction of either objects or people, or both. The children report spending each day waiting for the next "shoe to drop" and wondering what would set Robert off next.

Florence's Growing Confidence

Florence was remembered as having a fine sense of humour with a hearty laugh. Neighbours and relatives recounted that she was fun to be around. She was also strong-willed, as her interactions with Robert attest. One story about her revolves around her desire for a doorway in one of the many houses where they lived in this period. On having it explained that inserting a doorway into a completed wall was not easy, she took up a sledgehammer and broke through a section of the wall, finishing off the edges so she could easily walk through. That satisfied her.

As a younger woman, Florence had been compliant to the older Robert, avoiding conflict whenever she could. But as she matured, especially after she had children, and with the strong partnership with A.D., her willingness to follow Robert's orders waned. Slowly, she took to actively fighting back, ordering him to "leave her alone."

But, like all stalkers, Robert would not comply with Florence's demand, finding ways to intrude into Florence's and her family's lives. Robert's narrative was that Florence was having many affairs, she was an immoral woman, and his presence was needed to protect Pearl from following the same lifestyle. Robert did not attempt to explain why the same man was partnered with Florence year in and year out. Yet he

Margaret and Brian in front of Florence's prized car in 1956.

would not release her through a divorce, so he would never be done with her. Clearly, Florence felt powerless to ask for a divorce, since the legal grounds available to her would have been separation for two years, and he never left. As a lawyer, A.D. must have also determined that a divorce was not possible.

Meanwhile, Florence's confidence in her own abilities surged. She named and resisted every example of Robert's abuse. The children observed Florence throwing objects at Robert to force him to leave her house. On one memorable occasion, Margaret and Brian were outside sitting beneath a window when a bottle of mustard crashed through it and landed on the grass beyond them. As they listened, they were horrified to

Patsy as an infant in 1956.

hear Robert threaten, "I am going to shoot you." Florence responded, "I can shoot just as straight as you can! Leave us alone!" It should be noted that Florence had no gun. Florence was defending herself and her family in the strongest way she knew. And while Robert would not, or possibly could not, comply, he must have recognized that she would no longer be cowed by him. This was the last argument the children recalled between the two.

In 1956, A.D. bought Florence a car. This not only made her life easier in shopping for her family, it gave her freedom to escape Robert's demands and taunts. Robert, too, had a series of cars, all of them "held together with binder-twine." Neighbours reported hearing the familiar

Margaret, Patsy, and Brian in 1957.

clanging and creaking of Robert's car, a 1948 Chevy, from afar. He, too, had freedom to roam, therefore, and to track Florence and Pearl, if he felt that that were necessary, as he always did.

Florence's developing confidence and maturity arose from her relationship with A.D. and from motherhood. With Patsy's birth in 1956, Florence seems especially to have hit her stride. The early picture of baby Patsy on page 124 shows a happy, healthy little girl looking for approval from the camera. At the opposite end of the siblings from Pearl, Patsy also occupied a special place in the family constellation, the forever baby. Anyone who ever met her would use the descriptor "cute" where Patsy was concerned, and one can readily see why this was so appropriate.

Patsy was noted to have developed a quiet, watchful nature. She kept very close to her mother and loved to help her in the kitchen. Neighbours remember her as being like most children: she had many friends amongst the local children by her home, had sleepovers, and shared the occasional bit of candy. As one of the younger children, and because she was so agreeable, she was a great favourite in the neighbourhood. In the photograph above, we see Patsy hanging on securely to Margaret's hand as she pays close attention to the chickens around the coop. She was a curious, sweet-tempered child.

All of the children loved books, and especially stories of animals. Had Patsy lived, she might have chosen the natural sciences as a career. Along with her brother and sister, she carefully copied pictures from books, colouring them to improve their appearance. Florence scrounged books from every source possible so the children were kept occupied and learning.

Did Florence report her fears for her safety and that of her children to authorities while she was in the hospital? Robert's violence was certainly noted there. There is no record of her seeking help, and no one took any action to control Robert's increasingly bizarre behaviour.

There was a high degree of secrecy in the household regarding the marital breakdown, financial problems, and Robert's unsettling rants. This would have been due in part to 1950s norms where marital breakdown was kept a secret and, in part, to the shame Florence had been

Card written by Florence to her brother George in 1962. Sadly prophetic, it carries a double message: the pop-gun displays a "happy birthday" flag, while Florence expresses her anxiety "after such a long winter." Indeed, that winter had been endless for her with many cares.

made to feel for her alliance with A.D. Hall. Florence therefore would have been cautious about how much she revealed to anyone.

When family came to visit, Robert occupied the house as if he were part of the family, and A.D. found something to do away from home; when family left, Robert did, too, returning to his shack with no electricity or running water. The children called Robert "Dad" because Pearl did so, but never "Daddy." A.D., their true father, was called "Joey," and the children loved him unreservedly. Rarely did anyone other than family come to visit. By the early '60s, family visits stopped, too, as it became known that Florence and Robert were living apart.

However, as Robert's threats became more frequent and violent, we know that Florence called on the few people whom she felt she could trust. Florence wrote to both of Robert's siblings, specifically expressing her fears of being murdered. Both Gladys and Harold and his family visited at one time or another, but neither was able to break through the illusion of a functioning family that Robert (and Florence) created when outsiders were in the house. And like most abused women, Florence would not openly discuss the situation with either Gladys or Harold for fear of backlash from Robert after they had left. Nevertheless, the physical blows and verbal taunts increased. Florence must have felt increasingly desperate and alone.

The above card was sent by Florence to her brother George to celebrate his birthday. Her message reads, "I thought this card cute. It's the way I feel after such a long winter. How are things in Fort William. Peg and Brian are entering Festival on the 28th ... I'm well pleased. Drop a line sometime like to hear how everyone is? Love Sis." Florence had feared for her life for so long that she was now making jokes about being shot.

As this period wore on, Margaret became an essential support to Florence, who was trying to cope with a situation clearly becoming more dangerous by the day. In a conversation with Margaret, Florence sat staring out a window as she bit her nails in anxiety. She reported a nightmare in which Robert, sitting in a chair, was speaking to her disembodied head, which was resting on a table. Robert had many times threatened to shoot her in the head, and in her dream he had apparently done that, while also severing it. This was understandably shocking for a twelve-year-old child to hear, and yet it alerted Margaret to the depth of the danger in her household, possibly preparing her for when the final blow was delivered. It also speaks to the level of anxiety that Florence experienced in this phase.

Florence also confided in Pearl, now closer to her than in the past. This caused Robert to feel that he had lost his link with Pearl, that Florence had "stolen" her from him. Margaret was present during a threat-laden screaming match between Florence and Robert in which Florence noted that she had "told Pearl how the kids were born," undoubtedly referring to the parentage of the three youngest children. It was a strange turn of phrase, and therefore Margaret remembered it. Predictably, Robert was enraged anew, and countered with, "Pearl has turned out just like you." This was an ominous accusation, suggesting that Pearl, too, was a "lost cause," that there was no hope in "saving" her from the libertine lifestyle adopted by her mother, however hard Robert was trying to "correct" matters.

Robert was mostly well disposed to the younger children, and there are few accounts of his abusing them as he did Florence and Pearl. He seemed curious about the children and surprised when they displayed intelligence. At the same time, his idea of childcare was remarkably casual. On one occasion, Robert took Brian with him to visit Gladys. Soon after arriving, with no food having been offered, Robert and Gladys left for hours, with Gladys's dog in Brian's care. "Don't touch the dog," warned Robert. "Dogs have worms, and you don't want worms." But with nothing to do and nothing to eat, Brian happily patted the dog and ate the dog biscuits.

Where Pearl was concerned, however, Robert was anything but casual. He could easily become unreasonable, anxious, and angry, lashing out when she did not hold to his notions of acceptable behaviour. It was in protecting Pearl from Robert's anger that Florence found her own voice. If once she had meekly accepted his demands, she would do so no longer, for both Pearl's and her own welfare. As Pearl moved toward adulthood, the need to protect her became ever clearer to Florence, emboldening her.

Pearl's Developing Independence

Robert was particularly determined that Pearl should receive a good education directed personally by him, and thus avoid becoming part of the "ignorant riffraff" he found all around him. To accomplish this, he sat with Pearl as she did her homework each evening, with her frustration steadily mounting until she was often in tears. Nevertheless, it is clear that Pearl and Robert had a powerful bond and that she did try to please and placate him, especially where her academic progress was concerned. Pearl was a good student but, like many pressured children, she felt she could not measure up to his impossibly high standards, especially as they were communicated with his impatient shouting.

Over time, Robert succeeded in alienating Pearl as she, like Florence before her, sought to escape her unhappy home. It is safe to assume from this detail of their lives that Robert would have made just as poor a teacher as he made a minister.

As she neared adolescence, Pearl became even more restless. She would not avoid the local children, as Robert insisted because, he said, they were far beneath her. She made friends at school and was popular. She arranged to spend time with both girls and boys by meeting them at friends' places after school, and she often slept over.

Her school mates noticed her grace and intelligence. Friends remember her riding the bus — a quiet, attractive girl. In time, the overnighters turned into staying away for days at a time. As Pearl entered adolescence, she sought out more friends of both sexes and socialized freely with the "ignorant riffraff" Robert was trying to avoid. Boys also came to call on her. Family lore tells the tale of one young man who strode up to the front door when Robert happened to be in the house. Robert picked him up by the scruff of his neck and unceremoniously dumped him on the roadway. The boy did not return.

Others came around, all of them dispatched as quickly as they arrived. Pearl objected and resisted each time; Florence ordered Robert to "leave her alone"; A.D. tried to cajole Robert into more reasonable behaviour; the children cowered as each instance spun into violence; and

Brian, Margaret, Pearl, and Patsy in 1959.

Robert carried on just as he had done, "protecting" his daughter. He listened to no one.

One of Pearl's friendships in particular highlighted Robert's unhealthy and relentless obsession with his daughter's every activity and movement. In the 1950s, Pearl developed a caring and innocent friendship with a neighbour boy living nearby in Brighton. Both musically talented, they played the piano together, often Chopin; they sang duets and chatted about poetry, books, and popular songs — Pearl's favourite at the time was "Autumn Leaves." They laughed at jokes and funny long rhymes, such as "The Cremation of Sam McGee." Many decades later, this same friend described the young Pearl as soft-spoken, kind, intelligent, talented, and very beautiful.

Pearl in a photograph taken by George Fraser in the family home, 1953.

As teenagers often do, these two friends shared their dreams, worries, and concerns for the future. A.D., whom Pearl considered as her protector, shielded this friendship from Robert by planning outings for them accompanied by himself and Florence. However, Robert was closely tracking Pearl and this boy, always hovering as close as possible. Robert's sick fixation with his daughter did not go unnoticed. To her shocked friend, Pearl once said, "Sometimes I feel like I'm suffocating. I can hardly breathe or move and I will do anything to get away. My father is a dictator. He'll kill us one day."

When Pearl and her friend couldn't see each other in person, they exchanged letters by mail. One day Pearl's friend received a threatening letter from Robert stating: "If you know what's good for you, you will leave my daughter alone!" However, these two young people carefully

Pearl in a moment of happiness in 1955.

continued their letter exchanges until a second letter arrived for Pearl's friend: "If you know what's good for you, you will leave my daughter alone! No more correspondence!" Even after several decades, Pearl's friend remembers with clarity each word in these menacing letters. Most frightening was the fact that Robert was somehow intercepting and reading their letters. Alarmed, the boy's father took the letters to the police only to be met with this response: "Don't pay any attention to this. It's just a father protecting his daughter. It's not really a threat." But the boy's father did take it seriously and, before one visit, gave his son a broken paddle to use as protection if needed, saying, "If he comes for you, use this. It won't kill him, but it will stop him." Pearl's friend never had to use the paddle because, over time, these two good chums drifted apart and amicably went their separate ways. Nevertheless, for Pearl's friend

Brian, Pearl, Florence holding Patsy, and Margaret, seated, early 1957.

there was "no forgetting Pearl's gentle nature and the sweet memories and impact of this friendship."

In 1961 Pearl began another relationship with an early school chum, Fred Campbell, who worked at a local industry and had a car. The car presented a much greater threat to Robert's authority and ability to track her, since it allowed Pearl to be outside his authoritative circle for longer periods of time. But to Pearl, her relationship with Fred also represented escape and freedom.

Pearl quit school at seventeen that same year, took a bank clerk job in Brighton, and set up an apartment. After much searching, Robert found and confronted her in the bank. He forced her to quit her job in front of her co-workers. He then packed up her belongings and drove her home. The cycle continued and escalated: Pearl found in one apartment or another and physically forced home; Pearl verbally refusing his author-ity; Robert raging.

In the school photograph of Pearl below, the only one of her with a full smile, one can note her beauty and the sparkle in her eyes. We can imagine Robert obsessively nailing Pearl's school photographs to the walls of his shack, staring mournfully at them, as he felt Pearl slipping from his grasp.

On one occasion when Robert went in search of Pearl, he found her visiting at her boyfriend's home. Before he drove there to collect her, Florence insisted that Margaret accompany him, sensing that Margaret's presence would offer a modicum of control in a situation likely to become dangerous. Margaret herself remembers the furious drive to the friend's

Pearl, age sixteen, 1960.

house and Robert striding up to the door. As Fred's mother remembered it, without warning, Robert crashed through their front door and grabbed Pearl by the hair, dragging her outside. Margaret stood, watching in horror, as Pearl struggled to get away while Robert shouted at her, forcing her toward the car. Suddenly, he began bashing her head against the car door. He only stopped when Margaret screamed at him to stop, crying and trying to protect her sister from the blows.

Knowing that she needed help, Margaret ran to the house, only to find the terrified family taking shelter behind furniture and afraid to confront Robert. (It should be noted that Robert always carried loaded guns in his car, so the family's fear was well founded.) Margaret found the phone to call her mother but had never used a telephone before. She puzzled her way through the process, eventually reaching Florence, who came immediately. The scene presented to Florence was Pearl on the ground unconscious, with Robert atop her with his arms cradling her and Margaret standing near to them, crying. Florence demanded that Robert get in the back seat of the car, which he did, still dragging Pearl. With Margaret beside her, Florence drove them all home to the Colborne law office and summoned the doctor. A.D. managed to separate Robert from Pearl, and he drove him back to his shack in Castleton. The doctor's assessment was that if this were to happen again Robert would kill Pearl.

The warning signs of Robert's escalating violence were not lost on Pearl, and they were obvious to Florence, too, and yet neither had the means to escape his clutches. To protect Pearl, Florence found a way to take her to stay with her grandparents in Vancouver in their small apartment. Not surprisingly, this did not go well: Pearl was bored and frustrated by her grandmother's ceaseless moralizing, and especially so after Florence left to return home. One day, Pearl Viola found that her granddaughter had disappeared. Pearl had scraped together the airfare to return to Toronto, where she was met by her boyfriend, Fred Campbell. They eloped and found a small house in Brighton in which to live.

In a few months, it was obvious that Pearl was pregnant, and that resulted in escalating rage from Robert, as Pearl slipped further from his control. Florence, however, welcomed the news of the pregnancy, taking

This watercolour of rolling hills around Orangeville, Ontario, reflected the landscape around Gladys's childhood homes. Painting by Ada Gladys Killins. Courtesy of David and Suzanne Killins.

Gladys used objects close at hand in her still lifes: driftwood, gourds, potted plants, or scarves. Painting by Ada Gladys Killins. Courtesy of Brian and Elaine Killins.

This landscape of southwestern Ontario explores focal points, with the centre of the painting distinct with a view of gentle hills. The painting's margins are almost blurry, as if binoculars were used. Note the slash of bright blue for the sky. Painting by Ada Gladys Killins. Courtesy of Tim and Sarah Cook.

Sunny Field, 1935. This landscape, while of Ontario farming country, is reminiscent of the farmsteads Gladys must have observed as a small child in Alberta. Note the richness and density of the foliage on the right. Painting by Ada Gladys Killins. Courtesy of Graham Cook and Ankai Xu.

Ontario Farm Landscape. The farm on which the family settled after returning from the prairies might have looked very much like this one. Here, Gladys uses a technique she had perfected: the road draws the eye past indistinct foliage to a sway-backed farmstead, the focal point of the painting. Painting by Ada Gladys Killins. Courtesy of David and Suzanne Killins.

In this landscape painting from later in her career, Gladys experiments with rich colour and form. She looks down as if from the sky into the deep woods. The bright blue of the water would later be darkened, although she continued to favour the mint green of the foliage. Painting by Ada Gladys Killins. Courtesy of Brian and Elaine Killins.

In this still life from the 1940s, Gladys experiments with form, using corn husks and dried apples as a contrast to the smooth edges of a pitcher and vase. She returns here to her favourite hues of ochre, beige, deep reds, and teal. Painting by Ada Gladys Killins. Courtesy of David and Suzanne Killins.

This landscape study from the 1940s is unusual in its lightness and winter setting. It shows her mature palette of ochres, deep reds, greys, and golds, with the log structure anchoring the scene. Painting by Ada Gladys Killins. Courtesy of Sharon Anne Cook.

During the 1930s, Gladys experimented further with form and colour. Both this study, from 1934, and the one following are of northern Ontario scenes, possibly done while visiting Robert. Her composition is different in this first painting than in most of her landscapes. Here, our view is drawn to the aqua water to the left of the painting, with the trees on the right forming a linear stand. Painting by Ada Gladys Killins. Courtesy of Brian and Elaine Killins.

In this second study in the North, Gladys uses an arresting palette of cobalt blue tones for the water beyond the stand of trees. She also presents a fiery set of bushes in the centre of the painting, with the effect of muting the trees that frame the water and bushes. The beauty of the landscape is striking. Painting by Ada Gladys Killins. Courtesy of Sharon Anne Cook.

Georgian Bay, 1934. Gladys's experimentation with colour continued throughout her career. Here she contrasts white with bright colours in both the foreground and autumn-hued hills. Painting by Ada Gladys Killins. Courtesy of Brian and Elaine Killins.

This undated painting represents another departure in style by focusing so completely on rural buildings rather than on the landscape that sheltered and sometimes threatened them. One constant in this period was Gladys's emphasis on rural studies. Painting by Ada Gladys Killins. Courtesy of Kelly Carson.

This study of craggy rocks experiments with form. The shield outcroppings in the foreground are balanced by rocks of different sizes and shapes in the background. This landscape was similar to what Brian would have found on the relatives' pig farm. Painting by Ada Gladys Killins. Courtesy of Margaret Carson.

This painting is a study in both colour and texture. The angry, layered sky featuring both light and dark with an approaching storm is reflected in the landscape, both lit by the sunny portion of the sky and shaded by the storm. Painting by Ada Gladys Killins. Courtesy of Margaret Carson.

A grapery and fields with a stormy sky. Here as well, Gladys focuses on varied light levels reflected on the landscape from a variegated sky. The central field and grapery are well lit, while the foreground is in shade. Painting by Ada Gladys Killins. Courtesy of Margaret Carson.

This study of small-town Ontario in the 1950s makes more use of deep blues and greys than many of her landscapes. A characteristically stormy sky became one of her hallmarks. Painting by Ada Gladys Killins. Courtesy of Margaret Carson.

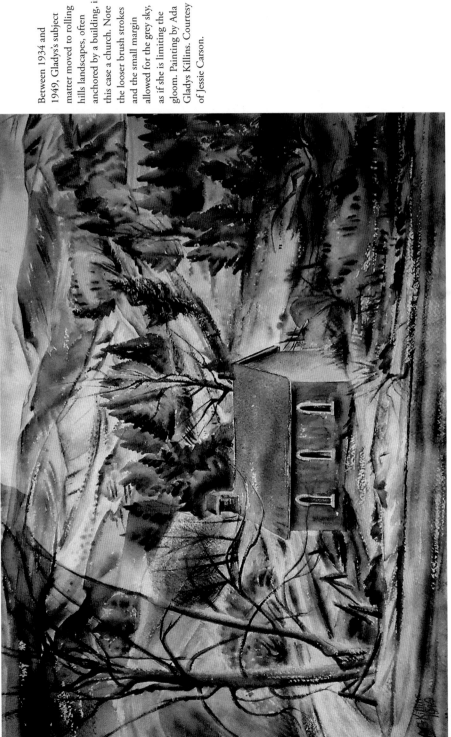

Between 1934 and 1949, Gladys's subject matter moved to rolling hills landscapes, often anchored by a building, in this case a church. Note the looser brush strokes and the small margin allowed for the grey sky, as if she is limiting the gloom. Painting by Ada Gladys Killins. Courtesy of Jessie Carson.

One of Gladys's cabins, likely built by Robert. Gladys largely ignores the sky in this study, as in the previous one, focusing her attention on the rock outcroppings. The purple-pink tones of the rocks mirror the cabin roof and stand in contrast to the muted colours of the rocks. Painting by Ada Gladys Killins. Courtesy of Margaret Carson.

This study of tree roots and branches from 1949, with no sky in evidence, stormy or not, explores movement and curves. Gladys further develops her technique of blurry foreground and sharply delineated roots and branches with splashes of lime green. Painting by Ada Gladys Killins. Courtesy of Brian and Elaine Killins.

This very subdued study from 1937 of two derelict buildings uses greys, deep greens, and ochre. While the house is the focal point, Gladys is also interested in depicting the late fall grasses and brush around the house. And, of course, she offers us another angry sky. Painting by Ada Gladys Killins. Courtesy of Sharon Anne Cook.

Compare the treatment of the bridge in this painting with that in the next one. Gladys reserves deep blues and greys for the tree trunks and branches and highlights new growth in the forest with lime greens and ochre. Painting by Ada Gladys Killins. Courtesy of Margaret Carson.

This late painting of a stream and bridge contrasts with Gladys's earlier studies of bridges in that this one is far more abstract. The watercolour is used sparingly, with a suggestion of looking through glass at the scene. Reflections abound. The technique used for the trees is a light stroke, blocking the colours of the trees in each case. Painting by Ada Gladys Killins. Courtesy of Brian and Elaine Killins.

Still life with bottle, dried apples, and art books. The bedraggled poinsettia and the dried apples create a sad theme of disintegration. Painting by Ada Gladys Killins. Courtesy of Margaret Carson.

Spring marsh scene. Deciduous trees in a flooded area are profiled against rolling hills. Gladys, with her dog in tow, always painted close to her home, since she did not drive. Painting by Ada Gladys Killins. Courtesy of Kyle and Elizabeth Carson.

Study for *Old Dam at Glen Cross*. A finished painting on this subject was recently included in an exhibition in Niagara-on-the-Lake. Painting by Ada Gladys Killins. Courtesy of David and Suzanne Killins.

care to maintain the bond between herself and her oldest daughter. With Pearl so close to her own home, Florence worked hard to maintain a strong relationship with her, and Pearl, too, welcomed this new, adult mother-daughter relationship.

In April 1963, Robert offered Pearl and Fred a house he had built on the property. He wanted to have them immediately at hand so he could continue his stalking from his shack. Pearl was uncertain about placing herself so close to Robert, but as her pregnancy proceeded, she and Fred felt that the proximity to Florence would be wise. In addition, the house offered free rent and additional money occasionally from Robert; eventually, a deed to the house and land was promised, which Robert did not own but lied that he could arrange this. In exchange for living there, Robert monitored their lives rigorously, sneaking into the house and marking bottles of alcohol to chart how much they were drinking, despite the fact that Pearl did not drink alcohol.

By accepting Robert's "generous" offer, Pearl exposed herself and Fred to an even more concerted stalking regime. Stalking is now a criminal offence and is defined as following another person against his or her wishes and harassing the victim. Although the crime was only formally recognized in the 1990s, people demonstrating an obsession of this kind have been known for many years. In 2014, more than two million Canadians were victims of stalking.[3] Often, but not always, the object of the person's delusion is thought to be in love with the stalker. Although "star-stalking" has received much of the recent press with disturbing examples, it is now generally accepted that the most common object of the stalker is a woman attempting to leave an unsatisfactory relationship, which has often been characterized by abuse. It operates as a naked form of male domination. This was the case with Robert's obsession in stalking Florence. Pearl became a stalking object when, in Robert's deluded opinion, her marriage to Fred demonstrated too much independence from his influence.

A debate exists about whether stalkers are mentally ill or merely neurotically obsessive. Some classification systems distinguish between psychotic and nuisance stalking. However, whether or not stalking signals a mental illness, it is now generally accepted that stalkers often react violently against the object of their obsession when the person does not reciprocate their interest or passion.

Stalking tends to occur either at the start or the end of a relationship, and the duration of the stalking also varies. In Robert's case, the end of his relationship with Florence in the mid-1940s signalled the start of the stalking. And however angry he remained with Florence, he tried to maintain a positive link with Pearl. Stalking can carry on for years, as it did with Robert. In this instance, Robert stalked both Florence and his daughter for at least sixteen years.

There is one major way in which this example of stalking departs from the norm. Robert compulsively stalked Pearl even more than he did his estranged wife. He did so with an apparent inability to stop or even interrupt his obsessive cataloguing of where Pearl was at all times. In order to be as close as possible to two women who did not want him near them, he "dropped in" almost daily to establish Pearl's whereabouts. When he did not find Pearl with Florence, he followed her trail by interviewing anyone who might have seen her. Then he descended on her, demanding that she return with him. When she refused on several occasions, he beat her almost to death. When he could not physically control Pearl, as we have seen, he reacted violently. "Stalking is a gateway to murder,"[4] authorities suggest.

A.D. Hall's Death

As long as A.D. was alive and well, Robert remained partially controlled. This uneasy balance shifted dangerously in 1956, almost a decade after Robert had first tracked Florence east and walked forcibly back into the family's life. That year, A.D. had a serious heart attack and spent some weeks in hospital. He was rarely again able to summon the strength to intimidate and reason with Robert.

After Robert's vicious beating of Pearl in 1962, and her mother's and her departure for Vancouver to hide from Robert, A.D. cared for the children on his own. He was clearly very unwell, and Robert took that opportunity to come and collect the two older children on most weekends. He pressed the children into service in whatever building project he embarked upon, expecting the children to get their own meals and to otherwise care for themselves.

A.D.'s death in 1962 was the source of deep grief for the whole family. It left Florence both abandoned, with Robert at close hand, and destitute. Margaret and Brian were heartbroken and worried. But Patsy was the child who showed her distress most clearly. She concerned everyone with her response: her naturally quiet nature became almost dazed. Everyone noticed it, despite the tension in the home. Her school principal observed that both he and her teacher noticed Patsy's sadness and anxiety, and that they tried to show her extra attention to bring her out of her shock. Neighbours, too, saw her grief at the deep loss in her life.

Florence and the children felt shunned by the Colborne community at A.D.'s funeral. On a visitation to view his body, Florence divulged to the children that A.D. was their natural father. In retrospect, neither child was surprised by this fact, since they had always related to A.D. as a parent. But they continued to call Robert "Dad" together with Pearl, even though they now were alerted that Robert was not related to them.

At the funeral, Florence, Margaret, and Brian were forced to stand at the back of the church, unacknowledged and ignored. They stayed for a while and then left in tears. Florence had not been prepared for this reaction, and it was a reminder of how fragile her social standing was within the community. No members of Florence's family attended.

Now that Florence and the children no longer had any claim to the law office where they had been living, Robert arrived late one night and moved Florence with the remaining children back to Castleton. There was no choice. Because A.D. and Florence were unmarried, he feared placing her in his will. However, he did buy property around the province in Bannockburn, Castleton, and other locations as one legacy on which Florence could draw. Unfortunately, because of Robert's menacing presence, she could not sell any of the land, and it eventually went to the various municipalities for back taxes.

Colborne, 1960. A.D. Hall's law office was the last building in the row at the extreme right. The family lived in the two-room law office for three years.

Florence and the children did not return to the old family home. Robert had managed to burn it to the ground in the previous months; thus, the housing was makeshift and meagre. Robert controlled the only money coming into the household from social assistance. It would not have been much, but Florence had no resources at all of her own, and her parents chose not to contribute to her financial welfare. Now Robert was in control again, walking at will into Florence's space, intruding on Pearl and Fred's lives, making ever wilder claims and demands.

Where were the police during this extended period of terror for Florence? At the time, there was no term to describe what Florence was experiencing. Domestic matters stayed in the home for Florence and many other women, particularly in rural settings like hers. It was not until twenty years later in 1982 that the issue of domestic abuse was first raised in the Canadian House of Commons by MP Margaret Mitchell to a chorus of laughter and hoots from other members of Parliament.

Patsy, Florence, and Brian, 1963.

Because Robert had not yet acted on his threats, the police would have told Florence that there was nothing they could do to help her.

What of her friends? Florence did have some friends in the community, and they might well have guessed at the abuse, but they were also without means to extend protection to her without raising Robert's ire, possibly endangering the whole family.

What of school authorities, who must have seen the effects of the domestic tension in the children? By 1962, Pearl had quit school. The two older children were relatively cushioned by the loving parenting they had received from Florence and A.D. But Patsy was younger and much more vulnerable. The principal of her school told us that he and her

Castleton Elementary School, 1930.

teacher identified anxiety in Patsy early in her schooling, but that there was virtually nothing to be done to help her unless physical wounds were present. He expressed his deep regret after the fact that he had been so powerless.

And why would neighbours not report Robert's abuse? Community members we interviewed observed that the watchword was "a man controls his own castle" in this period. But children noticed the violence before their parents did. One story comes from 1958 when a school friend of Margaret's was permitted to sleep over, a very unusual circumstance in the household. The children were giggling in their beds when Robert shouted at them to be quiet. He followed up by arriving at the bedroom door, taking off his belt, and whipping Margaret and Brian. The guest was so shocked that she never returned to the house for any reason. Still, when she recounted this to her parents, nothing was done.

As 1963 wore on, Gladys was increasingly concerned about her brother's emotional, physical, and mental stability. She corresponded with Florence, who herself was ever more worried about his mounting violence and irrationality. Unable to make any progress with letters to Robert, Gladys accepted an invitation to come and visit the family in Castleton. Once there, she and Florence continued their correspondence with Margaret carrying notes back and forth between her aunt and her

Florence, April 2, 1963, one month before her murder.

mother. But these messages, comforting as they likely were to Florence, did not prevent the coming catastrophe.

And then, there was the final straw for Robert: Florence found a new partner in a retired miner, Tom Major. Closer in age to Florence than either A.D. or Robert had been, the couple was devoted to each other. In early 1963, it was clear that Florence was pregnant with his child. The couple talked about moving away with the younger children to start a new life. They began making plans to leave within the month.

In Robert's opinion, the end had come.

CHAPTER 6

Murder Premeditated

———

Where the Murders Happened

In May 1963, there were two houses and two shacks on the family's land: Florence Killins's house, a shack occupied by Gladys Killins, the Campbells' house, and Robert Killins's shack. An old farmhouse had also stood on the same piece of land, but it burned down in 1962 when Robert overheated the leaky coal oil stove in the living room or the kitchen wood stove. This fire was during a period when the family had fled to live in the law office in Colborne, and Robert had moved from his shack into the farmhouse. After the fire, there was suspicion that Robert had intentionally burned the house for the insurance money. "The heat was so intense nothing was saved," reported the *Cobourg Sentinel*. It was reported by neighbours that Robert was frantically running around breaking the windows, which fed the fire. Later, it was discovered that Robert had saved his guns, ammunition, and some of his sister's paintings from the fire and secreted the guns and ammunition around the property. The paintings he placed in the shack where Gladys stayed when she visited in

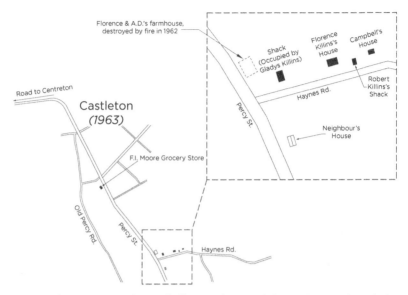

Florence & A.D.'s farmhouse,
destroyed by fire in 1962

Shack
(Occupied by
Gladys Killins)

Florence
Killins's
House

Campbell's
House

Robert
Killins's
Shack

Road to Centreton

Castleton
(1963)

Percy St.

Haynes Rd.

Neighbour's
House

F.I. Moore Grocery Store

Old Percy Rd.

Percy St.

Haynes Rd.

Map of Castleton, Ontario, with inset of Killinses' residences, including two houses and two shacks.

May 1963. Robert was taken to hospital for burns.[1] However, he refused to stay. Later, he turned up in Colborne, seeking A.D.'s help in securing insulin. Unwell himself, A.D. died a week later.

As can be seen in the floor plans below, Florence's house was a bungalow with a full basement. Press reports would describe all of the houses as "shacks,"[2] but this was inaccurate. The family had lived in the basement of Florence's house until the main floor was completed. It had been built by A.D. for Florence and their children as well as Pearl before she married. It had two bedrooms upstairs and one in the basement. A kitchen nook, bathroom, and combined dining/sitting room completed the main floor. The basement had an open cistern, a wood stove, and storage for canned goods as well as tools. The stairs to the basement had a landing from which one could view the upstairs hallway. In 1963, Florence and her partner, Tom Major, lived here with Margaret (twelve), Brian (ten), and Patsy (six). While the house had two doors, the front door, leading into the living area, was never used. All foot traffic went through the side door with the stairwell to the basement.

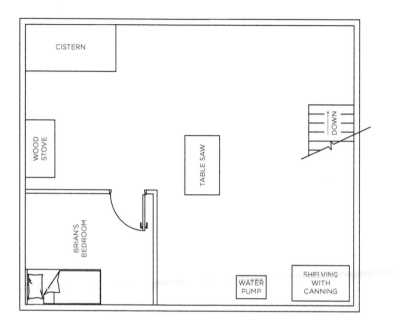

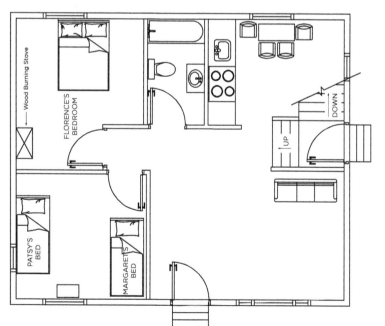

Main floor and basement plan of Florence Killins's house.

A one-room shack, which in the map on page 146 is called the "Shack (Occupied by Gladys Killins)," was located to the extreme west, facing Percy Street. This shack existed before the family moved to Castleton and was separated at a distance from the other buildings. It had a rough woodshed attached to the entry. A flimsy door closed the shack off from the woodshed. The shack had two windows, of which one small one faced the main house. Anyone coming to it would have surprised the occupant unless that person expected the visit. The family used the cabin for storage, and it was cluttered with objects. This is where Gladys and her dog, Taffy, stayed while visiting on May 2, 1963.

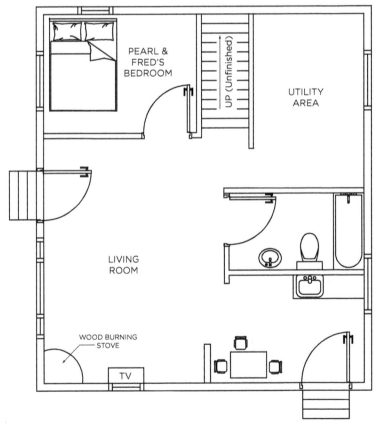

Plan of Pearl and Fred Campbell's house.

Between Florence Killins's house and the Campbells' house was a second one-room shack, built and occupied by Robert Killins. It was the second shack he had built himself on that land. The first had been abandoned because it was too far away from Florence's house for him to be able to monitor movement in and out. This shack had a wood stove but no electricity or plumbing. It was constructed of cheap fibreboard and had no insulation. It measured about ten feet by fourteen feet, providing enough space for a bed and a table, about the same size as a prison cell. Rough bookshelves held books and scattered notes, and Robert's long-time problem of hoarding papers was evident. Robert's shack was a fire hazard. Spikes were hammered into the wall, and on these, Robert hung papers by puncturing them. His food was almost exclusively tinned, which he ate without heating the contents directly from the can. From this vantage point, he could monitor everyone coming and going to both houses as long as he kept his door open, since his shack had no windows. In winter, he put up with the discomfort. He had the option of living in the shack where Gladys visited, but if he had done so he would not have been able to monitor Pearl or Florence.

The final structure, the Campbells' house, had been built by Robert to sell, despite the fact that the land on which it stood was not owned by him, but instead was in Florence's parents' names to protect it for Florence. This house was also a bungalow with one bedroom, a kitchen nook, bathroom, and dining/living room with a wood stove. A TV sat against the same wall as the exit door that everyone used. This house also had a front door, but it was never opened. The house had an unfinished attic. There was a stairwell to this space, which could have been renovated into a second story at some point, and indeed, this is how the house was reconfigured after the murders. In May 1963, that upper area was empty. The stairwell created an enclosed closet with a door at its base where the water tank was located.

Until it burned in 1962, there was an old farmhouse on the land. It is shown with dotted lines in the map on page 146. The family lived here intermittently from the late 1940s. However, Robert's intrusions into their living space regularly drove them away to other refuges: to Orangeville,

149

Brighton, and Colborne at one time or another. Once they were installed in most of these other makeshift homes, Robert tracked them down and built a shack as close as he could manage to the main residence. The only place where this did not occur was in the town of Colborne.

News reports after the murders complimented Robert on his building abilities: "A skilled carpenter, he built eight houses during that period [of fifteen years in the community], four of them for his family." This was inaccurate. In truth, he built a shack and the Campbells' house only, the latter of which was basic and small. In addition, he took commissions in the community to build structures for others.

The Events of May 2, 1963

On a warm, sunny midafternoon on Thursday, May 2, 1963, Robert starts out in search of each member of his family. He wants to place everyone and check their plans for the evening so he can find them when the shooting starts. Why did he choose this day? We will never know, but we can guess: within the past week, Florence and Tom Major had announced that they would soon leave Castleton with the children and move to northern Ontario. Pearl was close to the end of her pregnancy, and once she delivered her baby, her attention to Robert would be even more deflected than it already was as she focused on creating her own family apart from her father. Robert's health was declining by the day, and he must have wondered whether he would have the strength to "even the score" if he waited another week. His estranged wife and daughter were now irrevocably lost to him, as would be the children with whom he had bonded after a fashion. His sister had taken his wife's side, and he must have felt betrayed by this slight. Despite arguing furiously with Gladys, he could not make her see his perspective, so he gave up and took to brooding. By the afternoon, his mood had lightened remarkably, and he smiled and laughed at everyone he saw. His plan was set, and he was systematically mapping his family, ensuring that he knew where everyone was located.

3:00 p.m.: Robert encounters Margaret outside on the path between Gladys's shack and Florence's home. She is carrying one of the many notes between the two women as they struggle to understand the level of danger Robert presents. Robert smiles at Margaret, seemingly happy, an act so unusual she has remembered it for the intervening fifty-nine years. "Do you need anything?" he asks. She shakes her head, wondering what he means: money? food? a ride to a friend's? She responds that she needs a note for school because she was absent for the day. (The other students had gone on a field trip, but there was no money for this extravagance for Margaret.) Robert emits a high-pitched laugh almost like a shriek at her request, startling her. Robert rarely smiled or laughed aloud. He carries on walking, leaving her musing over his question and his odd response.

4:00 p.m.: As he moves toward his shack, Robert sees a cluster of neighbourhood children playing outside. The group includes Patsy, aged six. When the gathering breaks up, a neighbourhood friend of Patsy's, Lorraine, and Patsy head to the main house to ask Florence if Patsy may sleep over at Lorraine's house that night. "No," says Florence, "We need to be up early tomorrow morning." The two children continue playing together until suppertime. It is a lovely day and the children are enjoying the time outside.

5:00 p.m.: Florence and Gladys are meeting quietly at Florence's house to discuss their worries and a possible escape plan. Both are alarmed at Robert's recent threats and by his change of demeanour, in which he appears to be happy, even ebullient. They have trouble making sense of this change, and are on edge because of it, but even after three hours of intense discussion, they do not arrive at a final decision of how to defend themselves if he moves against one or the other woman. Tom Major has been party to parts of the discussion; he is well aware of Florence's and Gladys's heightened fears.

5:15 p.m.: Robert drops off groceries to Pearl and Fred and hands some cash to Pearl. Pearl observes that this is the first time he has done something of this nature and attributes it to the imminent birth of her baby. Passing by, Brian observes that Robert has removed the roof rack from his old car. Why, he wonders?

5:45 p.m.: As Lorraine and her sister Elaine walk home together for supper, they, too, meet Robert, who gives the children two bags of candy, an unusual act. They accept it, noting with surprise his ammunition belt around his waist with bullets for his shotgun. The children are used to Robert's strange behaviour and guns hidden under the blanket on the back seat of the car. They take the candy home and hide it in their bedroom. Within a couple of hours, Lorraine has eaten one piece of her candy and a terrible stomach ache comes over her. It is later suspected that the candy has been laced with rat poison. Their mother confiscates the candy in the morning after hearing of the tragedy at the Killins residence and throws it out.[3]

6:00 p.m.: Margaret has supper with Pearl and Fred at their house. She stays on after dinner to help with the dishes, visit with them, and watch TV. Everyone is tense because of Robert's oddly positive tone of late. However, what is to be done but carry on? There had been years of strange behaviour, and one learns to live with a threatening presence.

7:00 p.m.: Margaret leaves briefly to walk back to the main house, but she returns to spend the evening with Pearl and Fred. "I wanted to be out of the [main] house," says Margaret. "Robert had been wandering about much of the day and he made me nervous."

9:00 p.m.: Gladys has returned to the guest shack where she is staying after supper and an exhausting discussion with Florence and Tom Major. She is trying to monitor Robert's increasingly bizarre behaviour, but she has given up for the night. Afterward, someone reports having heard a car backfire at that time on the road, near to the house where Gladys is staying. It is actually Robert's shotgun being fired at Gladys's guest cabin door, which lies in splinters on the ground. Gladys and her dog, Taffy, have each taken one shot to the head, killing them instantly. This might have been from the shotgun or from one of the pistols. Aside from the splintered door, and cyanide and strychnine pills and shells strewn around on the floor, we know nothing about the circumstances of her death. We don't know whether she tried to talk Robert out of his plan, if she tried to protect herself and her beloved dog, or whether she was caught so by surprise that she was defenceless in every way. The splintered door suggests that she locked herself in the cabin, refusing to face Robert, but that because of the cabin's small size she was unable to find cover. Whatever that interaction was like, there was an extraordinary amount of blood, which eerily remained there until the house burned down four years later.

9:30 p.m.: While Margaret is visiting Pearl and Fred, Robert arrives and asks Pearl if she is planning to go to bed early. Everyone is surprised at both the question and Robert's presence. He normally goes to bed with the setting sun since he has no electricity or plumbing in the shack. He stays for a few minutes to watch part of a program. Fred offers Robert his galoshes, and they are accepted.

9:35 p.m.: Margaret walks from Pearl's house back to the main house. She walks past Robert's shack, where he is standing outside and is able to see her entering the house. Patsy is already asleep in their room, and Margaret begins to get into her pyjamas. Florence enters Margaret's bedroom and says, "You had better go to bed. Aunt Gladys has gone to bed already." Florence draws this conclusion because there are no lights on in Gladys's house. She has not heard the gunshots.

9:45 p.m.: Robert enters Florence's house and goes directly to the basement, an unusual route and time for him. He finds ten-year-old Brian in his bedroom. He has *never* been in Brian's bedroom before and his presence startles Brian. "Do you need anything, like a drink of water?" he asks Brian. "No, well, good night," replies Brian from his bed. "Goodbye," says Robert and leaves. Brian muses over the word used: "Goodbye" rather than "Good night." Robert ascends the stairs and leaves the house.

9:47 p.m.: Florence has washed the dishes and now she is sitting in the kitchen at the little table under the window with Tom Major. Florence sits at one end of the table, and Tom at the other. Without warning, Robert bursts into the room with a hot plate he has retrieved from his shack. He throws it on the table in front of Tom with the comment, "See if you can fix that!" He asks Tom to change position so Tom's back is to the entrance hall. Tom complies. Robert moves back to the entrance and immediately pulls out two handguns and crouches in the doorway like Marshal Dillon in *Gunsmoke* while shouting, "Now I've got the both of you!" Florence shouts, "Oh my God, Bob, no!" He shoots Florence in the head with one of the pistols and gets Tom in the back of his neck with the other. The bullet enters behind his ear and exits near his jaw. Florence falls back in the chair, having been shot in the forehead.

Tom jumps up to see gunslinger Robert still crouched in the doorway. Disregarding the obvious danger, Tom advances on Robert and strikes him with his fist, pushing Robert off balance and backward onto the floor. Tom grabs Robert's wrists and forces him to walk backward into the living room, where they fall on the floor. He wrestles one pistol from his grip, aims it at Robert and fires. Nothing happens. Throughout this, he is shouting at Robert to let go of the second pistol. Robert holds on with a vice grip.

Robert and Tom continue to struggle in this fight to the death.

9:48 p.m.: Margaret has taken off her socks and shoes, and she is unbuttoning her blouse when she hears screams and two shots from the kitchen. She does not register the sounds as shots but thinks that something heavy has fallen. She also hears banging. Patsy stirs, and Margaret tells her, "Stay here!" as she runs as fast as she can down the short hallway to the kitchen. There, she sees her mother with her head at an unnatural angle resting on the back of the chair. She knows that she has been shot. It takes a second to register the horrible truth, but she has no time to take in the rest of the scene. Robert and Tom are struggling on the floor, scratching, smashing, raining down blows. She recognizes the sound she heard as being Robert's gun hitting the floor.

This was the banging she heard, as two bodies struggled to regain control of the precious guns, grunting, swearing, bleeding, sweating. Robert frenzied; Tom fighting for his life, aware that if he loses he will end up like Florence. Now he is fighting for Florence, too. Tom has knocked one gun free, but he cannot wrest the other from Robert's iron grip. There are four hands on the single revolver. Margaret flies down the three steps of the short landing by the back door and out to safety. It feels as if she is running faster than humanly possible as adrenalin courses through her system. She runs in bare feet straight ahead, heading for Pearl and Fred's house to get help and warn them.

9:48 p.m.: Brian is in his basement bedroom, already in bed. He knows that Robert left the house, but when he hears jingling, the sound of the buckles that Robert wears on his galoshes, he knows that Robert is back. He hears screaming and two loud bangs. Bounding up the stairs, he stops on the landing, which has a view of the hallway and kitchen. As he stands rooted in horror, he sees his mother sitting with her head against the wall, gasping for breath. Brian stares at the scene, horribly confused. Brian stands staring at the scene until he notices the guns in Robert's hands. Tom Major is struggling with Robert on the living room floor. Had Tom Major not attacked Robert, very likely both children would have been shot next, since Robert has taken pains to know where every family member is located. But Tom's attack is a surprise. Robert is not expecting resistance of any kind, and this throws his plan into disarray.

9:49 p.m.: As Brian takes in the scene, Tom, on top of Robert, calls to him, "Brian, call the police!" Brian responds, "I will!" Robert is able to muster the strength to respond to this: "No, don't!" Brian flees through the same door Margaret has just used but turns to the right as he runs across the road, making for the trusted neighbours, the Days, the only people he knows who have a telephone. He arrives in pyjamas and hysterically bangs on the door, where Peter Miller and Jean Day are watching television. Miller boards at the Days' home and is Brian's teacher. In barely coherent phrases, he describes the scene to Miller and Jean, with now all three in the living area, and begging for the police to be called. Peter Miller picks up the phone and calls but cannot get anyone to answer. Finally, he makes contact and is told that they will be at least an hour. Castleton has no officers in the area. The OPP are busy. Jean Day calls her father-in-law for help, since her husband is driving a rig. She is lumbering around as she is nine months into her pregnancy. Within the next few hours, her baby will be born.

9:50 p.m.: Fred Campbell enters the main house, and both Robert and Tom stare at him. Tom asks him to help him. Robert warns him, "Don't you dare." Robert continues, "Help me! He is trying to kill me!"

Fred, confused and terrified, leaves the house. When asked at the inquest why he did not respond, he replies, "I don't know." He also stated that a gun was pointed at him.

9:52 p.m.: Tom is finally able to get the second gun out of Robert's grip. Robert lies on the floor, insensible. Tom knows that this is his chance to finish this horror. He turns the gun on the murderer. Like the first one, this one does not fire either. It has jammed in the melee. Tom looks at the gun in disbelief.

He is bleeding heavily and beginning to lose consciousness, but he is awakened from his stupor by Patsy's screams. He runs into the kitchen to find that Florence's body has slid off the chair onto the floor. There he also finds Patsy, who has emerged from the bedroom. She is crying, rooted in terror, and unable to move. Tom realizes that he must call the police and a doctor. But he also must track Robert on his murderous rampage.

He returns to the living room to see Robert struggle up from the floor and pick up a two by six piece of lumber, left around from some repair. Now he is swinging it at Patsy. He hits her leg, and she screams in pain. Tom places himself between Robert and Patsy, shouting at Robert to get his attention, which is focused on the child: "Don't hit her again or I will kill you!"

A hammer is lying on the table. Bleeding profusely, Tom grabs it and jumps on Robert, smashing him in the head repeatedly with it as he tries to wrest the piece of lumber from Robert's hands. Neither man speaks, as they struggle, wild-eyed, sweating, and in a frenzy. They are exhausted, slippery with sweat and blood, almost bestial. Only adrenalin keeps them going, along with Robert's deep anger, which can only have been driven to this through fury. Soon both men are bathed in blood along with their sweat.

9:55 p.m.: Finally, Robert collapses. Tom is equally exhausted and seriously wounded. He slumps to the floor but steadies himself. He knows that to fall will mean his death, even as Robert lies gasping and moaning. He steals a glance around the room, surveying the destruction. Chairs are overturned, and there is blood everywhere. The hammer has left a bloody trail across the walls and cabinets as Tom plunged it into Robert's head over and over again. He can barely look at Florence, but he knows she is dead. He becomes aware of silence, where Patsy had been crying in the kitchen. He sees that she is now silent, lying close to her mother. He must find help for Margaret, wherever she is. He has not noticed Margaret escaping into the night. Tom turns back to Robert, prone, quiet now, seemingly helpless, and perhaps dead.

As if rising from the dead, Robert regains consciousness, staggering to his feet in the blood-bathed house. He lurches out the door as Tom watches in amazement.

Tom pulls himself together, grabs both handguns, and runs as fast as he can from the house toward Castleton. He is bleeding freely from the bullet wound to the neck. Unsteady on his feet, he might pass out at any moment. Tom runs, his only thought getting help. Sprinting across fields, avoiding the road because he fears that Robert is right behind him, looking over his shoulder at the murder house, Tom arrives within minutes at the F.I. Moore grocery store. He crashes through the door like a banshee out of the night. Tom is shaking uncontrollably, waving the guns around as the story spills out of him. He needs a doctor, and he asks Mr. Moore to call Wilfred Hockney, who has a car. Mr. Moore runs to tell his wife and family in the house about the murders. Mrs. Moore calls the police. Tom is so frightened he cannot stand still.

He runs from the store to the Hockneys' house, on the next street behind the store. He is still shaking and now weeping, banging on the door. Mrs. Hockney and her two daughters bring him into the house. Wilfred is out with the car, but they will harbour him until Wilfred returns. They turn out all the lights and sit in darkness with the doors locked, half expecting the killer to arrive in pursuit of Tom. Tom lowers himself into the crawl space of the basement, and he sits there in shock, waiting for Wilfred to return with the car. The children bring a bandage for Tom's neck. Tom is bleeding dangerously.

Bathed in blood and perspiration, Tom looks almost as if he has taken a bath in the grim mixture. Tom breathlessly tells them of Florence's murder, the hand-to-hand combat, and his escape, with Robert having exited from the house and now is who knows where. Maybe Robert was dead from the hammer wounds to his head?

After a long wait, Wilfred Hockney arrives home, and Tom is scooped into the car to be taken to Cobourg Hospital.

9:57 p.m.: Covered in blood, breathing hard as he tries to focus his eyes and his attention, Robert staggers out of the open door into the night. He lurches his way back to his shack. He has caches of ammunition and firearms all over the property, in his car, and his shack, and he is now in search of one of these to finish the job he started.

9:58 p.m.: Peter Miller learns that Brian has an older sister living in another house down the road and suggests that they walk there to get help since the police will take another hour. It is eerily quiet, and they are both thinking that this terrible event is now over. With the lack of streetlights, they walk in almost complete darkness, but Brian knows the way. As they move past Robert's shack, Brian sees a shadow moving between Robert's car and the shack and whispers this to Peter. When they arrive at Pearl's house, Fred unlocks the door and meets them in the kitchen. Pearl immediately joins them from the bedroom and puts her arm around Brian. Margaret hears the voices and, too terrified to be left alone, she makes a move to follow her sister into the kitchen but her body, still violently shaking, forces her to sit back on the bed.

9:59 p.m.: Pearl, Fred, Peter, and Brian stand huddled together in the middle of the small kitchen, anxiously talking and trying to make sense of what has just happened at Florence's house. To their horror, through the window they see a figure crossing the yard. It is Robert, bloodied and terrifying. He has found more ammunition in his shack and his car. How could this be? Now he is advancing toward the house. There is no time to react. Fred lunges to lock the door, but it's too late. In less than a minute, the door flies open.

10:00 p.m.: Robert almost falls inside and immediately begins firing his shotgun. Peter shouts for everyone to hit the floor, but the shotgun does that for him. Robert shoots into the middle of the huddled group. The blast sprays around the room with tremendous force. "He just opened the door and fired," Brian will recall at the first inquest. Robert uses one barrel of a double-barrelled shotgun. Pearl screams, "You killed him!" as Brian is blasted out of her arms. The blast is so powerful that Brian is lifted off his feet and slammed into the far corner, dropping to the floor: his ears are ringing, he sees stars, his hair is singed, and his scalp is scraped from front to back. Pieces of plaster are scattered around him and, in shock, he wonders if these plaster pieces are parts of his skull. Tufts of hair fall away in his hand. Feeling his head, he finds he is still intact.

Peter is lying injured in the middle of the floor and, when he makes a movement, Robert aims the shotgun at him. Peter raises his arm and puts his hand up to shield his face, shouting, "Don't shoot me!" But Robert fires the second barrel of his shotgun to blast Peter again, badly injuring and burning Peter's arm, chest, and shoulder. This causes Peter to temporarily pass out. After regaining consciousness, Peter stays still while covered in his own blood and plays dead for another few minutes. Even though Fred is injured from the first blast, sustaining wounds to his shoulder and neck, he moves Pearl, also injured, into the utility room to hide her from Robert.

10:02 p.m.: Brian is still rooted to the floor in the corner. He has watched in horror as Robert shoots Peter for the second time. He assumes that Peter is dead. Brian is vaguely aware that Fred and Pearl are no longer in the kitchen. While standing directly in front of Brian, Robert reloads his shotgun by removing old shells. Brian does not look up to make eye contact with Robert but stares unblinking at the shells being loaded. Brian is so close that he can clearly see the numbering on the bullets. He wonders, bizarrely, if it is possible to stop the shooting by jamming his fingers into the end of the shotgun, as he has seen in TV cartoons. Knowing he is completely trapped because Robert stands between him and the outside door, Brian feels his heart pounding hard and rapidly. As if in slow motion, Robert reloads and aggressively locks down the shotgun. He readies it to fire again and moves toward the next room. He ignores Brian and Peter, perhaps thinking they are dead. Robert shifts his attention to hunt down Pearl and Fred. His job of killing is not done.

With gun raised, as if hunting animals, Robert now stalks his daughter, the great love of his life he has worked tirelessly to control and mould into the perfect child.

Brian now realizes there is clear access to the open door. A sharp jolt of adrenalin propels him through this door, out to safety, and into the pitch black night. He is running faster than his body can keep up and soon falls, smashing face first into the side of a hill. He is stunned by the impact but his body, legs, and bare feet feel nothing as he jumps up and continues to run down the gravel road. He does not look back. Again, he finds the Day house and bursts through the door to find Jean Day waiting while her children sleep.

Brian tells her that Peter Miller has been killed. They are both terrified. They turn off all the lights, lock the door, and hide huddled together on the floor in the back bedroom, listening to the continuous sounds of gunshots. They remain hidden until the shooting stops and the police arrive.

10:03 p.m.: Regaining consciousness and thinking that Robert has gone, Peter Miller pulls his bloodied body up. He is not thinking straight, but he notices blood all over the room. It is his. He, too, stumbles out the door, in shock, and runs. Almost immediately outside the door in the black and foggy night, he loses his footing and falls. He puts his arms up to break the fall, but they are dead weight, shredded by the shotgun blast. Peter barely registers this as he goes face first into the ground, almost knocking himself out. As he goes down, he hears a blast. Robert has heard him exit and he rouses himself from the couch onto which he has fallen in his own faint. Robert pushes himself up and follows Peter outside. He shoots at him again but misses, in the blackness of the night and because of his increasing weakness. Peter is up and running again for his life toward the bush at the back of the property. He knows there is cover there in the darkness and the brambles. The ground is uneven, and he falls, rises, and falls again. He looks like a drunken man, although one bleeding to death and believing a killer is chasing him.

At the closest farmhouse, the Taylors discover him at the door, pounding and screaming for help. "I don't know how he ran so far," said Mrs. Taylor. "His jacket was soaked with blood, and blood was even streaming down his pant legs," she told reporters.[4] A friend of the Taylors, Jim Hess, gets him into the car to take him to the hospital. On the way, a tire blows. Without even stopping, Jim carries on, driving on the rim. To the relief of both, they arrive safely.

10:04 p.m.: Robert lowers the shotgun. He doesn't think he got Peter. He stares into the darkness, wondering if he will hear a cry of pain or a scream of agony. Nothing, just the faint sound of someone running through the dark. He stops for a second. He turns around and re-enters the house.

Pearl is hiding in the hot water tank closet, and Fred is nearby behind a partition. Pearl repeats over and over, "Lord, please help me," as much to herself as to Fred. In turn, Robert takes aim at the hot water tank closet door, shooting several times. Pearl is behind that door and is mortally wounded. Before she collapses in a bloody heap, she manages to call out to her husband, "Help me, Fred, help me!" She crumples to the floor in a pool of blood as Fred struggles onto his feet to help her. Robert ignores Fred and walks unsteadily past the couple up the stairs to the empty second story. He is reloading as he walks. Who is he looking for?

Meanwhile, Fred is able to escape and runs for help. He has his car keys, but finds the tires flattened, likely by Robert. He knows that Pearl needs immediate help. He says his goodbyes and runs into the night, following the road, until a car stops for him, taking him to Trenton hospital.

10:06 p.m.: Robert, now an automaton, begins to descend the stairs one heavy step at a time. Blood is pouring from his head wound into his eyes, and he slips halfway, stumbling and slumping down the stairs. He settles for a moment. He is exhausted. But he does not stop. He rights himself, stands, and falls again. Determined and driven by his hate, he pulls himself up again, leaving behind blood on the railing, stairs, and walls. He is looking for Margaret.

During the horror downstairs, Margaret has been looking for her escape. Margaret tells herself to run. She can't. There is only one way out and Robert is blocking it. She looks around the room frantically. Can she jump from one of the windows? She has no time and could not get the window open in any case. She does what children do when they want to hide. Margaret crawls under the bed.

Margaret is frozen in fear, listening. Listening to murder. Listening to screams and shouting. Listening for the man who many think is her father as he kills her older sister. Listening in the silence as Robert climbs the stairs. Listening as he falls, rises, and falls again. Will he stay down? Is it done?

It is not done.

She hears the clink of the buckles on his boots. She hears him grunting and panting and making animal sounds. She hears it all and it is coming closer.

It is no easy fit. The space under the bed is shallow and, although she is thin, she must push the bed up before getting under it. A bit at a time, she wedges herself into place, lifting the weight of the bed onto her back. Trying to be quiet, holding her breath. She is under. There is no room, and the mattress board is jammed into her shoulder. She waits in silence. She waits in the dark shaking. She knows there is no escape if he finds her.

She has her head turned to study the door. She does not want to look but she can't move her head. Robert's feet appear. They stop. She can only see up to his ankles. He says nothing but the faintest of sounds suggests he is scanning the room. In a rush, he seems to collapse beside the bed. Margaret is staring back into his bloody face, only centimetres away. She forgets to breathe. She is utterly undone, believing that the end has come for her, too. She can do nothing to escape. She is trapped under the bed and about to be murdered.

She stares into Robert's glassy unblinking eyes. He continues to stare back at her, his bloody cheeks pressed to the wooden floor. In the darkness, Margaret does not know that he cannot see her. She moves her eyes to his hands, which are visible. Bloodied, they are curled around the shotgun. Finally, after what seems a long time, Robert struggles to his feet and lurches out of the house.

Margaret draws a deep breath.

10:07 p.m.: Robert shuffles outside, seemingly insensible. But, no, he continues his evil work. He stumbles over to the cars on the property and fires several shotgun blasts into their tires. He then fires into the walls of the houses in a frenzy of anger. He is not done.

Robert re-enters the main house and finds Patsy's body in the kitchen. He drags it through the house and, inexplicably, takes her outside to the back porch. Despite a trail of blood, it is a small body, and the blood mixes with all the other blood in the house. Patsy will not be found for another day.

10:30 p.m.: Margaret has been hiding under the bed for what feels like hours. Likely she has blacked out during this ordeal. She listens to the ongoing gunfire, which eventually stops. When there is complete silence, she slowly eases herself out from her hiding space. She walks out of the bedroom into the main room that is bathed in blood. Puddles of blood pool on the floors, and she carefully picks her way around them. She is still in bare feet and partly undressed. Holes have been blasted through the walls. Margaret still feels the effects of the shock. Her mind sends a series of electric shocks to her body as she negotiates her way through the house. Expecting to see dead family members, she finds none. She does not realize that Pearl's body is behind her, under the stairs in the hot water tank closet. She stumbles in her stupor and steps in a warm pool of blood, recoiling in horror. As she moves carefully through the house, she realizes that the television is on with a blaring laugh track. She stands and stares woodenly at the television for a few seconds before running out the door.

10:35 p.m.: Margaret stares toward Robert's shack, and she sees his car parked in front. She hears a car door slam. But he is not in it. Where has he gone? Is he still gunning for her?

10:36 p.m.: Now Margaret, too, is on the run and still in bare feet. The grass is wet. It washes some of the blood from the soles of her feet. This is replaced with mud. She is trying to find her way to the neighbours on the other side of their house, but she repeatedly loses her way at the back of their property because of the heavy fog and black of the night. And the terror has done strange things to her perception. She should know the way to the neighbours', but she feels muddled and unsure.

She falls repeatedly, with the panic growing. She cannot seem to find her way out. She runs into a barbed-wire fence at some speed, cutting herself badly. But the fence gives her the reference point she needs. She can see the way now. As she unclenches the barbed wire from her hand, she stumbles and falls on her face, injuring herself further. Yet on she struggles, moving slowly toward the road she knows will lead her to the Days' house. She hears Robert's car door slam shut. She knows where he is and where she is and where the Days' house is, too. Her path is clear now; she just has to find the strength to get there. She runs down the gravelled county road in bare feet, toward the house. She does not fall on the stones as they bite into her feet.

Margaret is drawn to the light of the house. She bursts through the door and is met by an officer with his gun trained directly on her. She collapses.

10:38 p.m.: Robert drags himself into his car after shooting randomly at the black night, walls, cars. Is he hallucinating or clear-headed but weak? Whichever, he pushes himself onward through malice. He has done what he planned to do, and now it is time to escape — where? To the woods somewhere? To one of Gladys's cottages in the north? He has folded about three thousand dollars into his clothing; he has enough ammunition to hold off any assailant for a good while, if he can just stay conscious long enough. He is struggling because of the beating he has taken to his head, the exertions over the guns, and also because he has poisoned himself with strychnine, rat poison.

Robert manages to get his old car started and he slowly leaves the property. As he picks up speed, he holds a shotgun out the window as if searching for someone. As he draws onto the highway, a police car moves slowly into position behind him. Another police car speeds up and draws in ahead of Robert. These are the reinforcements finally arriving from Cobourg, Hastings, and Brighton. Several of the out-of-town police are lost when first arriving in Castleton; they have to ask directions at the local store. While the police had warned they would be an hour to arrive, the urgency of the call, no doubt passed on by terrified neighbours, sends them converging on the crime scene. Robert is driving his rattletrap car at speeds estimated to be between five and twenty miles per hour, weaving erratically across both lanes. The cortège moves onto the highway toward Centreton, just beyond Castleton. A cavalcade of police follow him, and police in the lead car see an officer lean out the window and begin to shoot at Robert's car.

Robert is unaware that he is leading a parade of police cars.

10:42 p.m.: F.I. Moore and his family are now standing in their yard beside their store. They have been alerted to the murders by Tom Major's arrival forty-five minutes earlier. Mr. Moore hears Robert's approaching car clanking along the highway. He shouts to his family and others to flatten themselves on the ground. They drop in terror.[5] As Robert's car passes with the police cars behind him, everyone watches in fascination. Robert is driving still with the shotgun sticking out of the window and aimed toward the Moore family. Soon another police car speeds along, and the family wordlessly points in the direction that the cortège has just gone.

10:49 p.m.: At an intersection near Centreton, west of Castleton, two police cars overtake Robert from two directions, forcing his car into the ditch. Robert has travelled about seven kilometres in his foggy state. Some of his head wounds have stopped bleeding, but others continue to drip down his neck. He lies at a strange angle in the front seat, with the car now in the ditch. In the vehicle is a sawed-off, double-barrelled shotgun with more than fifty shells strewn about. Add to this arsenal a Biretta twenty-two calibre automatic pistol and an automatic nine-millimetre Cold Commander, loaded with nine shells in the clip, both of which were taken by Tom Major.

Just then, Bill Pratt, principal of the Castleton school, is returning home from the theatre.[6] He encounters police cars, sirens, and lights. He slows his car and drives past the scene. There are several police officers who usher him along. As he passes in the night, he sees Robert's car in the ditch, with the driver's door hanging open and feet sticking out. Robert has slipped into a coma with the shotgun still propped in the driver's window. The massacre is over. It will be determined that dozens of shots have been fired by Robert over the course of the evening.

It has taken just under two hours from start to finish. But the preparation took far longer. The family had seen something coming for years.

CHAPTER 7

Aftershock

———————

Life and Death Arrive at the Hospital

Staff at the Cobourg General Hospital worked overtime that evening.

Tom Major had been taken to Cobourg hospital with a life-threatening neck and head wound. The bullet had entered by his neck and departed close to his jaw, so some reconstructive surgery was going to be necessary. By the time he arrived there, he knew that he was safe from his terrifying ordeal. He also knew that Florence and Patsy were dead. Relief was mixed with grief.

But finally, he could step back from the confrontation of his life. He spent time in hospital as his wounds began to heal, visiting the children every day, grieving with them for their mother and Patsy, and now, as he discovered, for Pearl and her aunt Gladys, too. After a slow recuperation, Tom managed to carry on with his life. Seven years after the event, he was still working in the Cobourg area.

Peter Miller soon arrived with gunshot wounds and burns to his hands, arms, and neck, suffering from the most serious wounds of any who survived. He was immediately taken into surgery, where there was fear that he would lose his hand. His family was contacted and rushed to the hospital to be with him. His father reported: "All we know is that Peter tried to get the gun, but he couldn't get it."[1] This twenty-year-old first-year teacher had been through a horrific night and he was sedated to start him on his long healing journey. He did not in the end lose his hand, and at the end of a year's recuperation he made a full recovery. He moved to Burlington and taught for one more year before starting on his degree at university.

Fred Campbell was admitted to Trenton Hospital with shotgun wounds to his shoulder. Separated from the other victims, he was alone until his family was able to reach him. Further, he had the burden of knowing that Pearl and the baby were dead. Fred was left "destroyed" by Pearl's murder, taking years to recover from the trauma, if indeed he was ever able to manage this.

Robert was brought in, thrashing around on the stretcher. He had been pulled from his car stuck in the ditch in a semi-comatose state. Handcuffed and bundled into an ambulance, he was transported to Cobourg hospital. After carrying out his campaign of terror and murder, wrestling with Tom Major, and blasting people and tires and walls with his shotgun, he was still not becalmed. In a frenetic state of arousal, covered in blood and sweat, he raved and struggled to get off the stretcher. He actively fought the staff as they tried to x-ray his head, so they could only guess at the diagnosis. If he were to meet death that night, he would not go quietly. In the hours after his admission, restrained and guarded by police, he fell into a deep coma from which he did not awaken. He died the next day, twenty-two hours after his rampage had begun.

Next into the Cobourg hospital came Brian and Margaret, both in shock and barely clothed. They had been kept by the Days at their house until Robert was captured. One after another, the police who had cornered Robert in his car found their way to the Days. There were at least five officers at the Day residence when John Day returned from his trucking job that evening. He found his house encircled by police cars, lights flashing. In an era before cellphones, he was out of the communication loop. This must have presented quite a shock to him.[2] The baby born during that night of horror has described how the recounting of those events became part of her family's identity.

As Brian was being debriefed in the kitchen by Orrin Day (John's father) and the police, Margaret was in the living room being treated for shock by a doctor. She was sedated for the drive to Cobourg. Orrin Day told Brian the details of the family members who had been murdered. But no one told Margaret.

The police car carrying the children to Cobourg hospital passed Robert's car being towed out of the ditch. Both children looked out the window in stunned silence, asking themselves where Robert was by that time, and fearing that they would find him at the hospital.

As the children were helped from the police car, a nurse and doctor ran toward them, ushering them into an elevator. As the nurse looked down at Margaret's hand, still bleeding from having fallen against the barbed-wire fence, she asked anxiously, "Another gunshot wound?" On closer inspection, she found that these were surface wounds, although impacted with mud and dirt. Relief.

The news of his family having been wiped out threw Brian into a silent fog. He assumed that Margaret had also been told the terrible news, but in fact he was bearing this alone in his silence. They were placed in the same hospital room as they huddled together against the terror they had endured. Brian was unable to speak, and Margaret had no idea of the terrible knowledge he held until the next morning.

Margaret's confusion was made worse by the staff's decision not to discuss the murders with them on their admission. This seems a questionable strategy in retrospect, and yet it was in keeping with notions of the day of how to treat traumatized patients. The code of silence sealed Margaret off from the inexperienced staff's support, and it kept Brian trapped in his bewildered shock.

The staff caring for Margaret and Brian was comprised of young nurses and doctors who understandably struggled in communicating to them what little information they had received. None of them had likely ever experienced or worked through a catastrophe of this magnitude with orphaned and traumatized children in their care. Unfortunately, their vague exchanges with the children served only to further confuse them. At the same time, everyone was caring, and the children recognized this, even in their dazed state.

In the morning, the staff arrived to bustle the children into baths. Brian was particularly bothered by the residue of the gunshot in his hair, and he asked for shampoo. A kindly older nurse offered him a bar of soap, insisting that it would do the trick nicely. Brian complied. Both of the children were relieved to have the dirt and blood washed from them. They were given hospital pyjamas to wear, and they recall being much more comfortable once they were bathed and fed. Neither had been inside a hospital before, so the institutional food was a surprise, albeit something safe to talk about.

The doctor and nurses finally broached the topic of their family's deaths with the children. Brian was surprised that Margaret had not been told the sad news. Margaret reacted with tears and the need to talk about it, but Brian was still wrapped in his silence, unable to communicate at all. Both children worried the staff with their reactions: "The little girl is sobbing hysterically, but we are more worried about Brian," a nurse told a reporter from the *Toronto Daily Star*. "He really is too quiet — shocked into silence."[3] It took days before Brian broke down and cried. Brian's eerily quiet suffering continued through the first inquest a few days later when the coroner asked him to speak louder in answering questions. "Slim-faced, blue-eyed Brian Alexander Killins, 10, spoke in a low tone, hardly discernible. He was asked to say, yes, and not nod his head, when asked questions by Crown Attorney Deyman."[4] The silences continued into his new life in Calgary and became a hallmark of his adult identity. From there onward, "Brian was a quiet man, soft-spoken and reflective," remembers David. It was a personality quality forged in trauma.

On the same morning as they were told about their family's deaths, they were also alerted that Robert was alive and in the same hospital. However, the police were there to protect them, they were assured. This news terrified the children anew; they had a difficult time visualizing what was meant by this statement. No one had been able to protect them from Robert the night before; would he be able to wreak havoc again? The essential information of his comatose condition was not given to them.

The children had "escaped death by a hairsbreadth," as the *Toronto Daily Star* put it.[5] The *Star* was not wrong, and both children felt they were balancing on a knife-edge over an abyss. Their survival in contrast to the deaths of their mother, aunt, and sisters was already a dreadful burden. Why had they survived when their siblings, aunt, and mother had not?

Neither child had clothing or any keepsakes with them, and they were never permitted back to the family home to collect what they needed. Their past lives had completely vanished as a result of the previous night's events.

Who and where were their relatives, wondered the police and the medical staff? When quizzed about names and addresses, the children could only provide information that their grandparents lived somewhere in Vancouver and an uncle in Thunder Bay. They had no idea where Harold and Ethel lived, nor did they know any addresses, phone numbers, or even full names. Over and over, the police probed for details of the events of Thursday evening that the children could not provide. The neighbours were also interviewed, but neither could they offer much helpful information. Eventually the police created a spotty chronology of events, and this was the record from which they worked during the two inquests.

While he was still hospitalized, Tom Major daily made his way from his room to visit the children. His son steadied him. "He cried every time he saw us," reports Margaret. "He was so deeply traumatized, it must have taken months for him to get over the events of that night." Brian was permitted to visit with Peter Miller in his room, on the same floor as their own, but only in the company of a nurse. The protective staff worried about the children having no relatives with them.

Aside from Tom Major and Peter Miller, everyone else was kept apart from the children until their relatives arrived. This made for long, anxious days for the children with nothing but their own company to relieve the boredom. Looking back, Brian appreciates their enforced isolation. "The number of visitors we were allowed in the hospital was limited for good reason: there were reporters everywhere," reports Brian. The staff anxiously looked in on them, providing them with games and puzzles and bringing them other treats. "We spent no time in the halls. We did spend a lot of time looking out the window," remembers Brian. The stunned silence between the children continued, then and afterward.

The morgue was also busy that night and into the next day. The victims' bodies were formally identified by Wilfred Hockney, whose family had befriended Florence. Gladys's remains were collected from her cabin, Florence's body was taken from the kitchen of the main house, and Pearl's body was finally found in the hot water tank cupboard in her home. After an extensive search, Patsy's body was discovered outside, hidden from sight.

Reporters converged on Castleton to interview neighbours, some of whom were eager to speak to the press. Misinformation was piled on inaccuracy as reporters tried to ferret out the causes and progress of Robert's killing spree. Was Robert in charge of a cult? Some neighbours' imaginations were in full flight. One reported that the family was deeply religious, singing hymns at all hours of the night. Robert was presented as a doting father to his four children, regularly loading up his kids in his ramshackle car along with the local children to take them somewhere, including Niagara Falls in the middle of the night. All of these stories were fabrications, but they made for colourful articles in the immediate aftermath.

The newspapers also resorted to every melodramatic image they could conjure to feed public interest about the massacre and keep the story alive. Describing how Brian had been expected to play his cornet in the Northumberland Music Festival on Friday evening, the night after the murders, the *Cobourg-Sentinel Star* reported:

Danny Baker was the only one to perform in Class 94, Coronet [*sic*] solo, 12 years and under.... The other entry did not play. He was in Cobourg Hospital being treated for shock. Brian Alexander Killins, 10, was to have played the Petite Valse by Lotzenhiser…. Tonight, Brian and his sister, Peggy, 12, are family remnants shocked by the cold, relentless tones of death. Tonight four houses on the gravel road south of Castleton, Northumberland County, are bereft of light, etched solemnly against the sky.[6]

The narrative of the massacre presented in the newspapers was different from what our research indicates occurred. The fact that Robert was an ex-pastor figured prominently in almost every newspaper account: "A one-time United Church minister whose family was almost wiped out in a shooting spree at Castleton last Thursday night, died in Cobourg hospital Friday and took with him the secret of the bloody massacre."[7] The discordance of a minister of the faith slaughtering his family undoubtedly demanded to be noted. But what was the secret that was being sought? His motive? His actions? Possible associates? The rest of the newspaper accounts draw heavily on first-person reports to produce an outline of what occurred that evening.

The newspapers also quickly provided the reasons for the massacre: diabetes that was "out of control," a gangrenous leg, and "ill health for years."[8] The *Chicago Tribune* did allow that officers "had no immediate explanation for the shootings."[9] There was no accomplice; Robert was solely responsible. If the narrative seems to hold no secret, were the newspapers angling for an easy explanation — ill health — for why a former clergyman would butcher his family?

In reporting on Robert's health, the clear impression is given that his maladies made him violent. There is no evidence that diabetes results in aggression, and yet the newspapers leaned heavily on this interpretation. The possibility that an assailant could be motivated by anger, jealousy, and disappointment as well as misogyny to carry out femicide was never considered.

There is an almost sympathetic tone in some of the news reports regarding Robert's role in the family, if not in the murders themselves. The *Ottawa Citizen*, for example, noted (incorrectly) that the victims were "killed by shotgun fire in their home — built by Killins — beside his own shack where he lived alone on a side road near the village of 400 residents."[10] Another report explains that Robert had "moved here about 15 years ago, eventually building three houses for his family."[11] He was described as a "skilled Carpenter."[12] Aside from the fact that both statements regarding who built the houses and how many there were are inaccurate, what function do they serve? Are the comments merely to provide local colour, or do they try to describe a hardworking family man who "snapped" because he was ill and provoked? We conclude that the latter is the more likely subtext. Another explanation notes that "although he lived under separate roof, he apparently provided for his family. Neighbours describe him as a kind father. He always drove his children to and from school."[13] Although neighbours avoided and made fun of his strange appearance, several were quoted in newspaper stories as regarding the assailant as "a friendly, good neighbour."[14] Another newspaper offered this: "Mr. Killins neither smoke nor drank, and was said by Castleton neighbours to be [a] well educated, quiet spoken man."[15] These were the character references of a man who had just butchered his family.

It was not until the reports from the second inquest in late June of 1963 that Tom Major would be described as trying to disarm Robert to save the rest of the family, and in particular, six-year-old Patsy. Newspapers noted, almost as an afterthought, that Major struck Robert "in self-defence and in defence of two of the victims." But Tom Major was more than a lodger in Florence's home; he was Florence's lover and he tried to defend her and her children. Very likely, readers picked up that nuance in the accounts they read.

Did the interviewed neighbours express sympathy for Florence and the other women gunned down? Hardly. One observer acknowledged that Florence "was very nice to talk to,"[16] but did not seem to know more about her than that. Another neighbour observed, "They've been here for 15 or 16 years and I've never been in their house,"[17] as if this were somehow Florence's fault.

The narrative traced in the newspapers of the day, therefore, was of a sick man, but one who still managed to feed and clothe his family, and whose wife had for some reason turned him out of his own home. He lived in a shack, after all, which he had built with his own hands, along with better housing for his wife, children, daughter and son-in-law, and sister. Everyone had a decent house but Robert. Furthermore, his wife had a "friend" who was visiting at the time of the murders. Many readers would have concluded that Robert walked in on his wife and another man in a compromising position. Robert deserved better, and a woman like Florence who broke her marriage vows "deserved what she got," was the message.

Of course, these newspaper commentaries reflect the norms of 1963 in rural Ontario. But they also fed those notions of female victims "deserving what they got." This view was reflected in a conversation overheard by the children while in hospital. "He was wronged," said one person out of view, and the other grunted in agreement.

Reporting of this nature helps us to understand why it took so long to accept that the terms for divorce should be relaxed. Even more protracted has been the battle to recognize the horror of abused women trapped in violent marriages. For this is most assuredly a story of domestic abuse that escalated into a familicide. An unwillingness to easily accept this phenomenon extends even to our own period and country.

The Relatives Arrive

It took a couple of days for the children's grandmother, Pearl Viola, and uncle, Florence's older brother George, to arrive from Vancouver and Thunder Bay. Likely, the children's grandmother flew into Toronto on May 4, with George following by car from Thunder Bay. Grandmother Fraser was an intimidating and even frightening matron at the best of times, but with her daughter and granddaughters murdered, she was understandably upset and not the best of company for two traumatized children. Ira, Florence's father, had collapsed on hearing the news and he was in hospital along with Florence's brother, Bill. This left Pearl Viola alone to handle the tragedy in Castleton.

Unwell and alone but for her son George, she had to make the arrangements for travelling to Ontario and decide what to do with the surviving grandchildren. Harold and Ethel arranged for disposal of the bodies and for their funerals, which occurred on May 8 and 9. Pearl Viola should also have made arrangements for the sale of the houses and effects in Castleton, but she was too overcome to take on that task. Following time-worn patterns, Ira left everything entirely in his wife's failing hands.

The grief and anger made her even more abrupt with the children than they remembered from past visits. "Remember that we hadn't seen her for a couple of years, so she did not really know us as ten- and twelve-year-old kids. She was angry and stressed," remembers Margaret. She hovered over them on her visits, crying for the loss of Florence and Pearl, and confusing the children with her demands and accusations against the Killins family. Margaret reports that the children sat mute and watchful, hoping that her temper would not escalate. "I think we both really wanted more affection from her but we were also a bit wary of her," says Margaret. Pearl Viola's anger, particularly regarding the decision about where the children would live, alarmed both of the children. "In hindsight, she was not at all well physically, and we presented a complication to her that she had to solve," remembers Margaret.

The children concluded that something they had done had caused this catastrophe. Survivors' guilt is common in people who survive a disaster of this kind. Both children fought it and still are troubled by it. Margaret observes that "I think I still have it at times. The 'what if I had done this or that' was there for years. Replaying and changing past events are such human things to do, and, of course, I logically know that I could have done nothing to change the outcome."

For Brian, a form of survivors' guilt arrived with his fear that he would duplicate some of Robert's personality failings. This occurred because he had not absorbed the fact that Robert was not his biological father. He struggles to make sense of this in retrospect.

When I was a teenager, I discovered from Margaret that, indeed, Robert Killins was not my biological father and this, too, added to my inner calmness. I was able to put aside that sense of hidden shame and fear of my own temper and behaviour. I had been told twice as a child that Robert was not my father: once when my mother asked me to kiss my father goodbye as A.D. lay in his casket, and once by Tom Major in the hospital, after the shooting. The trouble was, we had always had two fathers, and I guess I took it figuratively so that I would feel better and not as a biological fact.

Realizing that he was not destined to replay Robert's script was comforting for him. However, there were several years of fearing his own responses before he reached this understanding.

Robert's brother, Harold, and his wife, Ethel, arrived slightly behind the Frasers on May 5. They were driven to Castleton by their son Wesley from Fonthill, Ontario. Wesley had been closer to Robert than anyone in the family aside from his siblings. Wesley admired and liked Robert, and Robert reciprocated the valued relationship to the degree that he was able to show affection to anyone. Wesley was the only relative who, with his wife Joan, visited Robert regularly. Curiously, these visits were only with Robert, never with Florence or the rest of the family. After the murders, Wesley and Joan tried to clean up the mess in the main house, taking on a task that must have been ghastly.

The Children's New Home: Contested Territory

Harold and Ethel suggested to Pearl Viola that the children be taken out of hospital to join the Killins family at Wesley and Joan's home in Fonthill, about six hours away. "Absolutely not!" thundered Pearl Viola. "Your brother killed my daughter and granddaughters, and you will have nothing to do with the children!" A blanched and shaking Harold tentatively asked what he proposed to do with Margaret and Brian. Pearl Viola declared that she would take them back to Vancouver and place them separately in foster care. She had already told the children that they would move to Vancouver. That was all she could think to do, she said. She explained that she was unwell and lived in a small apartment.

To Harold and Ethel, this seemed a very poor plan. Devastated by her accusations and carrying his own shock, grief, and guilt, Harold patiently set out his arguments to her. He acknowledged her age and health concerns, her history of coming to Florence's aid during terrible times, and the unspeakable horror of what his brother had done. But the children could not be abandoned to the foster care system, he stressed. Two wrongs did not make a right. There had to be some other way, and if she would grant him the time, he would find it. One way or another, he and Ethel would find suitable living arrangements for the children with family members, he promised. At long last, Pearl Viola relented, releasing the children to his care on May 7.

What exactly did it mean for Pearl Viola to "release" the children? Why did she have custody of them in the first place? Florence had left no will. Would a grandparent trump an uncle in childcare? We believe that Pearl Viola informally allowed Harold and Ethel custody of the children and that the local officials, having no alternative, permitted this decision. Because she did not contest the arrangements made by the only remaining member of Robert's family, the decision would have stood.

Then all of the adults made a serious error, causing the children even more distress. Having previously told the children that they would go to Vancouver with her, and before the children even met Harold and Ethel, Pearl Viola now informed them that they would be leaving with the Killinses and settling with someone in that family. But who? This surprising information was devastating to the children. They did not know Harold and Ethel, and being suddenly moved to the demonized Killins side of the family was terrifying. Despite Pearl Viola being a fearsome character, she was at least familiar. In Brian's words, the children felt "completely abandoned." Brian continues:

> Grandmother Fraser and our uncle George were the only family who came to see us by about the third day of our stay in hospital. We had no idea that the Killins and Fraser

families were discussing our future as we were told early on that we would be going to Vancouver with our grandmother. We did not know that Ethel and Harold had come to Ontario as we did not see them until after the decision was made for us to live with someone in the Killins family. Before the inquest, our grandmother abruptly told us about the change of plans as to where we would live. Her presentation was curt, matter of fact, and she would hear no complaints. She was almost angry — we wondered, "Was she angry at us?" We felt rejected and afraid and cried.

Margaret reflects on her grandmother's apparent anger and her influence on their demeanour:

When our grandmother Fraser first told us in her unemotional manner that we would be living with someone on the Killins side of the family, I also thought she was angry with us. We barely knew Harold and Ethel, and not at all the other relatives. We were understandably alarmed and frightened by this new decision. I look back now through the eyes of being a grandmother myself and realize that she was masking her emotions by presenting a firm decision-making exterior. Undoubtedly, it would have been more devastating for us to see her crying and sobbing while saying goodbye. We never saw her again after this visit as she died a number of months later. I am certain that my brother and I inherited and internalized Grandmother Fraser's seemingly stoic composure as a blueprint to face the next number of years.

Brian continues: "At this point, we only vaguely remembered Ethel and Harold, and I am sure that the feeling was mutual. Our interactions over the years were scattered and few. We begged to not go with Robert's brother out of fear. We now hated Robert, and Harold was his brother. Our grandmother left us no choice."

The children slowly came to terms with yet another disruption, this time into an unknown household with people they only barely remembered or, if the children were placed with other relatives, had never met. How can we explain this lapse in not including the children in plans for their own future? Harold and Ethel were undoubtedly themselves in shock, trying to make long-term arrangements in an impossibly short time period. They must have thought they were shielding the children from yet more pain by presenting them with a fully realized plan for their future. As well, this was an era when children were not consulted about life choices of this kind. Regardless, it was a serious mistake not to have at least briefed the children on the possibilities for their future since nothing was yet settled about where the children would ultimately live. This error was piled on others where the children were left out of essential discussions, feeding their perplexity and distress.

Funerals needed to be arranged for the four victims, although nothing was planned for Robert. In another misguided attempt to limit the fretfulness of the preceding days, Margaret and Brian were not offered the option to attend any of the funerals. A last-minute change of heart on Harold's part meant that the children stayed at Harold and Ethel's son's home alone during the funerals. Harold had been so overcome with emotion at the devastating loss of both of his siblings, he felt he could not attend. But at the last moment on May 8, he pulled himself together and left with the other adults. The children were warned not to go outside, so they spent the day wandering through the house, snacking, and worrying about their future.

Even the locations of the family's graves were kept from the children. Why? Concern for the children? Shame? General emotional overload for Harold, for everyone? After about fifty years, the far-flung burial locations were determined for all of the victims, including Gladys, whose body was sent to the Union Cemetery in Smithville, Ontario, near to the site of one of her cabins. Gladys was buried close to Caistor Township, where her family had first settled when she was a small child. Robert was buried in the Grafton Cemetery in an unmarked grave. No one attended his interment. None of the graves had markers, but these have since been laid. Robert's grave has never had a marker.

Grave marker for Pearl and her baby.

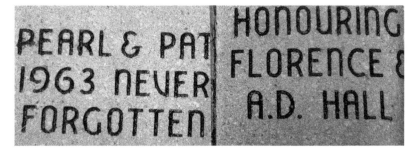

Memory stones placed in honour of Pearl and Patsy and Florence and A.D. Hall.

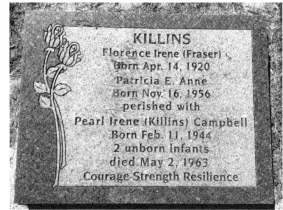

Grave marker for Florence, Patsy, Pearl, and the two unborn infants.

In death, as in life, the family's final resting places are isolated from one another.

Having had no opportunity to bid goodbye to their murdered family, nor any to collect any keepsakes from their former lives, the children became part of a bizarre tour of the homes and families of those relatives who had expressed interest in raising the children. In retelling this story, the survivors frequently broke into hoots of laughter because so much of it was ridiculous, a kind of Gothic child-shopping trip. But there was no humour at all in what they were about to embark on in 1963 — just sadness and puzzlement. But first, there was the inquest to get through.

CHAPTER 8

Taking Stock After the Familicide

———

In the first weeks after the initial shock of the murders had receded, life was by no means back to normal for Margaret, Brian, or indeed anyone connected with the familicide. First, the children were called to testify at an initial inquest. Because of the extent of Peter Miller's injuries, more time was needed before he could be asked to attend any public investigation. Nevertheless, the authorities knew that the children would soon be leaving the Castleton area, and their testimony was important to determine if there had been more assailants than just Robert. A second inquest was held after the children had left the area.

On the private level, there was a flurry of activity as Harold and Ethel assessed the options of a permanent home for the surviving children. The Castleton community itself tried to make sense of what had happened that night, ascribing reasons for Robert's rampage, some of which were accurate and some fanciful. In taking stock of the murders, a number of mysteries remain for which we have no answers. Perhaps there is still someone connected to these events who can provide information. Finally, in this chapter we present some of the facts around mass murders, femicides, and familicides, applying the research to this case study.

The Inquests

The first of the inquests, or coroner's juries, was hurriedly arranged and held four days after the familicide, on Monday, May 6. The five-man jury was comprised of worthy (male) citizens from Cobourg, none from Castleton. The presiding coroner and the crown attorney were also from Cobourg.[1]

It was thought that the inquest should happen as early as possible so the children could be removed to their new home, wherever that might be. The children were told that morning that they would be attending the session. There was a problem: they had no clothing other than the hospital-issue pyjamas. They recall bags of mismatched items being brought in by the nurses and doctors for them to try on. At long last, outfits were assembled for them, but the children felt self-conscious and uncomfortable in their borrowed garments. Shoes were a particular problem because Margaret had adult-sized feet. Eventually, a nurse contributed her shoes for the outing.

To avoid the reporters still camped out in front of the hospital, the children were led down long hallways, into the basement, through corridors, and, at long last, out of the back of the building into a waiting unmarked police cruiser. They felt almost like fugitives, as if they had done something wrong, as they obediently followed the police officer into the car.

Entering the courthouse was less fraught. There, only the principal lawyers and jury awaited the children. Tom Major, bandaged and looking pale, was there, too, with his lawyer. He gave the children a supportive little wave, showing that they were still in this together. No reporters were permitted in the courtroom, and the experience was less trying than anyone expected, including the children, who had been apprehensive. Nevertheless, the children were seated with police officers, far away from Tom, with whom they would have preferred to sit. This further isolation was upsetting to them, "retraumatizing," reported one. In retrospect, the children remember being glad to escape the confines of the hospital, even if for a short time.

A prime goal of the first inquest was to explore the events of the evening on which the familicide occurred, including the actions of any person other than Robert who might have been responsible for the murders. The thesis being tested was that Robert was solely responsible. Of course, Tom Major's attack on Robert was also under investigation. The authorities needed to ascertain if in any way Tom was responsible for any of the murders. Both children testified. Margaret responded with a firm no when asked if there was "any thought in her mind that Major had done any of the shooting." The children agreed that the firearms were Robert's and that he alone had carried out the carnage.[2] Brian was asked if anyone other than Robert was shooting that night. In his response, he recounted being able to see the numbers on the bullet casings as Robert reloaded his shotgun in Campbell's house after he had blasted Brian. Robert had delivered one blast, Brian reported, and then he prepared to shoot Peter Miller a second time. Brian was also asked about the gunfire he and Mrs. Day heard after he left Campbell's house. It was "as if a war was happening outside," he remembers many years later. The jury was satisfied with the explanations, and Tom Major was duly exonerated of any blame.

The second inquest was held six weeks later on Wednesday, June 19, to hear the medical reports of the perpetrator's death and to survey the events leading to the murders. The inquest had been delayed because of Peter Miller's slow recovery to a point where he could testify. By June 19, he was still in great pain, but he managed to attend and speak about the events. A full complement of reporters sat scribbling as the coroner, J.F. Leeson, presented the evidence.

It was confirmed that the cause of Robert's death was the hammering to his skull, which fractured it. Not surprisingly, Tom Major was judged by the jury to have acted in self-defence and in the defence of two of the victims, Florence and Patsy, as he struggled to disarm Robert.

The crown pathologist, Dr. F.L. Lawson, also reported some surprising findings. Robert was found to have ingested fifteen milligrams of strychnine at some point before or during the murder spree. The poison would have acted as a stimulant, he reported, because of Robert's diabetic condition, while his head wound would have depressed his actions. This helped to explain Robert's almost superhuman strength and endurance during the evening of the murders, and the fact that he could continue to hunt his victims long after his wounds would have been expected to have caused his collapse.

Further, police reported that Robert had at the ready more poison, should he have "needed" it. He had packed both strychnine and arsenic into nine-millimetre pistol shells that he had handy in a belt around his waist and stored in a homemade vest, with even more stashed in the car.[3] To those who knew him, Robert's ammunition/poison vest would not have been remarkable. Robert's collection of ammunition was large, with some of those nine-millimetre pistol shells containing shot. He also had more than three thousand dollars on his person. Clearly, the murders had been painstakingly planned in advance. All of this proved that while Robert had a disturbed mind, it was a cunning one, and that he had carefully planned his assaults, leaving his victims little to no chance. He seems to have given himself a variety of routes to escape, some physical, and others through death.

It was reported to the inquest that Robert had died the next day from skull fractures, which had caused a contusion to the brain. The hospital staff members were not confident in their diagnosis, however, since the patient had been rolling on the stretcher when admitted to hospital, creating difficulties in x-raying him. But even a superficial investigation of the many open wounds on his head, with matted blood and visible bone fragments, suggested that he had suffered multiple blunt-force traumas to the skull. The regional pathologist delivered his opinion that the direct cause of death was the concussion, exacerbated by his diabetes, gangrene, and poisoning.

The testimony traced the probable events of that evening for the jury, which was charged with deciding if anyone other than Robert Killins was responsible for the murders. Tom Major had been examined at the first inquest, and he was a principal witness in this one as well. In his testimony, he demonstrated more of the courage that everyone recalled on the night of the murders. He pointed out that he had not lived at the Killins residence for long: in fact, it had been less than a week. Nevertheless, although grievously injured with a neck and head wound, he fought valiantly for his own life and for the lives of Patsy and Margaret, the latter of whom he had thought was still in the house. He had seen Brian leave, and he had shouted to him to call the police. He did not elaborate on Patsy's position or condition, both of which remained shadowy at the inquest and for years to come.

Bidding for "the Boy"

When they found themselves in this maelstrom, Harold and Ethel were in a pre-retirement phase of life. They had raised their three children, only one of whom was still "in the nest" as they would have put it: their daughter, Sharon. Their lives were sedate, middle class, and currently focused on the needs of Ethel's mother, who lived with them and who suffered with dementia. Could they take on even one more child, and a traumatized one at that?

Harold and Ethel discussed taking Margaret back to Calgary with them, with the possibility of Brian following later. While they were fairly confident that they could raise Margaret, partly because Sharon was still at home, Brian would not have a companion. They felt that his needs would be harder to meet. But what would they do with him in the meantime?

This question was not easily answered. The lunatic plan of Pearl Viola snatching the children away from the Killinses in an apparent act of revenge and placing them separately in foster care was enough to shock them into immediate action and planning. Harold was deeply grieving, not only for the loss of his sister and brother and for the murders committed, but also for his inaction in the build-up to the crisis. He would later come to realize that nothing he could have done would have been able to divert Robert's intentions, and yet his new recognition of the family's years of terror depressed him.

Now, he and Ethel snapped into overdrive, telephoning even distant Killins cousins to see what options existed. It was clear to him that whatever placement they found might be temporary; the eventual arrangement would have to accommodate both children. Brian was still dazed and silent, worrying to everyone who tried to communicate with him. Despite their uncertainty about what to do about this in the short term, Harold and Ethel knew that the children could not be permanently separated.

In the meantime, Harold, Ethel, and the children stayed with Wesley and his wife, Joan. Brian remembers being drawn to Wes: "After leaving the hospital, we travelled with Harold, Ethel, Wes, and Joan. I had met Wes before and liked him. It helped to be with him." This is not surprising. As Harold and Ethel's oldest son, Wes was gregarious and kind, one of the most welcoming of the clan. He, too, must have been grieving because of his attachment to Robert, which stemmed from his childhood. As a bonus, Wes was gifted with mechanical skills, just as Brian was, too. They must have quickly established common interests that made Brian feel comfortable.

In the end, several distant Killins relatives stepped forward, offering Brian a short-term or possibly permanent home. As a strong boy of ten, there was potential that he could contribute to the family economy somewhere and be incorporated into another family. But no one offered a place to Margaret. Still, all potential placements would need to be explored. So began a series of excursions to visit these homes that would have been amusing if the life and welfare of a traumatized ten-year-old child had not been at stake.

First in line were wealthy relatives who offered a place to Brian as a companion for their son. Harold and Ethel seem to have thought of the placement as a short-term trial that might be followed up in later years. In visiting this family, it became clear that the parents were so combative, apparently with guns in the household, that this would not be an environment in which Brian could recover and thrive.

Brian describes the setting and characters:

> I was left for a stay with the wealthy family who lived in
> an upscale property on Lake Ontario. I didn't realize I was

being considered as a permanent playmate for the younger son. He was a bit spoiled and didn't take to having another boy share his toys. I remember his gas-powered mini Model T car we drove around the yard. He was miserable when I had a turn.

They took me to their church on Sunday, and I broke into tears during a hymn. This was the first tears and emotional release since the tragedy. It was music that brought the reality to me. I was taken out of the church by the older daughter, and she held my hand as we walked and talked. I felt an emotional connection with her from that simple physical contact but never told her and would never see her again. I wondered if at this point the family thought that I was too damaged for them to take on.

There was no room for Margaret in this placement, an arrangement now understood as unacceptable.

Of the remaining stops on this road trip, Brian says, "We continued with more visits. I have little recollection of them." Brian's lack of memory is helped by Margaret's very clear recollections — and her horror at the thought of her or Brian being abandoned there. A cousin kept a pig farm. Harold, Ethel, Wesley, and both children took one look at the subsistence life of the couple, the bareness of the house and outbuildings, the smell and size of the pigs, and realized that Brian would have been accepted mainly as a child labourer on the farm. It must have felt as if Brian had slipped into another dimension as a British "home child" where room and board would have been exchanged for labour.

The family had a daughter already, "the girl," as they called her, so they did not need another "girl" in the form of Margaret. What they needed was a "boy." The lack of first names was a clear tip-off that this "home" would offer nothing but misery to Brian.

Considering the limited options before them, and the obvious requirement to keep the children together, Harold and Ethel resolved to take both children into their own home. "We drove to Toronto and stayed with relatives, John Fry [Ethel's brother] and family. While there, the family was very, very kind to us and we felt like country bumpkins in a big city for sure. Then we flew from Toronto to Calgary. First time on an airplane … there were many firsts …" remembers Margaret.

Brian comments on his understanding as a ten-year-old of the many crises they had endured by that time:

> After the initial shock had subsided of finding out that we would go with Harold and Ethel, Margaret and I did what we always did — we coped with it. For some years, we had to deal with disappointment and tragedy. We were constantly moving and losing our friends and familiar surroundings. Our home and all of our belongings were burned. A.D. Hall had died, and we missed him terribly, and we saw the distressing mournfulness in our mother. We had experienced violent arguing and threatening between our mother and Robert, and, recently, we were learning to adjust to a new man in our mother's life and the thought of moving once again. We had witnessed our family murdered, and we narrowly escaped with our lives. We were frequently left on our own to entertain ourselves, but we had learned to cope.

"I do remember Harold explaining we would be going to Calgary and describing what it was like on the Prairies," remembers Brian. "Learning that I would fly on a plane excited me, and the trip on the modern DC8 jetliner was absolutely memorable. When we arrived in Calgary, it was shocking with so few trees, but we had been warned. It all seemed foreign. We drove to our new home in a modern car with seat belts, which we had never before used. The home was in the city surrounded by streets and sidewalks but virtually no trees. The house was spotlessly clean with carpets on the floor. It was as if we had been transported to a different planet. Every sense of our past and our identity was gone. We were starting a new life."

Life in Castleton Post-Familicide

Trauma existed in the community of Castleton, too. There was general uncertainty and even misunderstanding about what had caused Robert to resort to murder, as well as who had taken the surviving children and where they had gone. One common theme emerges from the collective memories from that period: everyone who lived there knows where they were on the evening of May 2, 1963. In response to a newspaper reporter's question as to what they believed had caused Robert to commit the crime, an unnamed neighbour speculated, "He must have gone haywire."[4] They could make little sense of what had happened and grieved for the orphaned children.

Other theories of Robert's motives circulated. Robert's status as a former clergyman was imprinted on many residents' memories and became part of the explanation for his rampage. For example, in a CBC Radio news report on May 4, 1963, a neighbour told Bill Harrington, the CBC reporter, that "several years ago, the couple [Florence and Robert] had often sung hymns together with the children and that it seemed a remote but happy family."[5] Neither Margaret nor Brian ever recall a family activity even tenuously resembling the singing of hymns. There was an assumption that the family was deeply religious and, until very recently, united. The implication was that religion played a part in Robert's motives. In fact, the family was not particularly religious, nor had they lived with Robert since arriving in Castleton.

The same theme was picked up with comments that all the children were faithful Sunday school attendees. This, too, is an overstatement, with the survivors remembering very occasional attendance and little support from home, except for Pearl, who Robert insisted would become religiously literate.

The familicide, especially its ferocity, is engraved in the memories of longstanding Castleton residents. Even in interviews about forty years later for a newspaper article, children of the area — now grandparents — remembered their astonishment at the many police cars in Castleton that night: "I have never seen so many police cars in Castleton before or since," remembered Pat Taylor Spencer.[6] One resident recalls "being made to stay in our bedroom with the lights out,"[7] signalling the terror that Robert was still on the loose. Another villager from that time recounts that "my dad told Mum to lock the doors. Old man Killins has gone nuts and is shooting his family."[8]

As journalists swarmed into the farm community, residents discussed their interactions with Robert, many of which were awkward but not troubling. They wondered what they could have done to support the family, grieving in particular little Patsy's death. One of Patsy's friends remembers: "Patricia was in my class. I remember how sad we were as we watched our teacher, Miss Massey, clean out Patricia's desk."[9]

Some residents, like Wilfred Hockney, considered Robert a friend. Irene and Wilfred Hockney had commissioned Robert to put an extension on their house, and they were pleased with the results.[10] They had particular difficulty understanding how any man could butcher his family.

Anxiety in the community continued the day after the murders as well. Joan Ferguson tells this story:

> It started out as a normal day with our ride on Perry's bus coming in from the Oak Heights area to the north. Upon our arrival in front of the school, someone entered the bus and we were told to go back home. There was a shooting and they weren't sure his whereabouts at that time. Basically that's what I recall, and when we were dropped at our home my parents weren't around as my mom was a schoolteacher in Fenella, and maybe Dad had gone to town for a grist or something. We didn't want to stay in the house because we wouldn't be able to see anyone coming down our side road and I remember thinking we might have to run away and hide if the shooter came around. Next day [actually, on Monday] we went back to school to hear the terrible news.[11]

By the time of the children's arrival on the school bus on Friday morning, the shooting had been over for about nine hours, with the perpetrator under armed guard in the hospital. But that did not quiet the nerves of the villagers, especially where the children were concerned. Considering the poor communication, in retrospect their worries are understandable.

Where the murders took place, the houses stood empty, with the interiors still coated in blood for some years. Marla Day remembers playing as a child inside Gladys's shack, the house almost immediately across from her own home. She recalls that by 1967 the shack had been emptied of everything but a few broken pieces of furniture. In their playing, she and the neighbourhood children ran through the shack and outside to the lean-to shed.[12] The land was fair game as a playground for local children. One resident recalls that "as kids after the tragedy, we would play and forage around the shack. Great for curious young country young'uns."[13] Other children were nervous walking past the houses, keeping carefully to the other side of the road and staring nervously at the remaining buildings. "Living and growing up practically next door to where this happened, it was often something that I thought of when going down that road."[14]

Not unexpectedly, there was probably looting of the houses in the months and years after that night in May. Money and various possessions disappeared, and keepsakes intended for the surviving children were gone when relatives searched for them.

The Amityville Horror movies of the late 1970s and early 1980s, in which a newlywed couple move into a haunted house that had been the site of a mass murder the year before, must have had particular resonance with the children as they grew into adults. In some instances, memories of the Killins familicide might have been supplemented by images from popular culture of the era, including this movie. This seems to have been the source of one neighbour's memory of Robert, quoted in a 2001 retrospective issued by the *Northumberland News*. The interviewee remembered Robert wearing a long trench coat in summer while carrying a shotgun. To the family's knowledge, Robert never owned a trench coat and he certainly did not wear one daily in summer with a shotgun in hand. This memory might have migrated from the Columbine murders, where one of the young men wore a trench coat while murdering people.

The main house remained empty for several years, as did the Campbells' house. Only a cursory clean-up had ever been done, and there would have been a lot of work left to make either dwelling habitable. Gunshot holes remained in the closet door of the Campbells' house. Eventually, new owners were found and both houses were occupied and improved.

Stories were told of hauntings in the two remaining houses. In one account, a friend of Margaret's and her sister were babysitting in the main house, watching television. The family had moved into the house on Halloween night of 1965. They report that hammering from the attic was so loud that they could not hear their program. The solution? "We turned up the TV!" reports Elaine McBride.

When the owners were asked if the house's history made them nervous, they responded that the presence was friendly. The family's two-year-old reported seeing "monsters" on the main floor of the house, although many two-year-olds would likely report the same about their homes. A second floor was added to that house and noises were heard from that location on occasion.

Another story comes from the Campbells' house. When the family who now occupy it first moved in, they heard a baby wailing night after night. Terrified of the sound and worried for her and her family's safety, the woman recounts that she tried to find the source of the sound and perhaps calm the phantom. She stood and spoke toward the ceiling, saying, "It's all right now. You are going to be okay." The baby quieted and they have not heard from it since.

Neighbours reported their belief that a curse overshadowed one of the death houses. As evidence, they noted that one of the men living there contracted cancer at an early age; another developed blood poisoning. Both men died.

In 1967, the cabin where Gladys was visiting and Robert's shack both burned. One account by John Day credits this act to neighbours wanting to rid the area of an eyesore and "a grimly silent reminder of sad and horrifying events."[15]

Family members report that they felt "smeared" by the murders, that their very name was cursed. The name *Killins* is distinctive and eerily close to naming the events of that day. One relative who carried the surname felt that she was shunned at work because of Robert's rampage; another felt that he carried it as a badge of shame for some years, avoiding the topic of the murders if it ever arose in conversation. A third considered changing his surname to escape the taint. Brian asks, "So why didn't I change my name after I found out [that he was not a Killins but a Hall in parentage]? Many times I thought of it. When Harold was alive, I felt as though it would be insulting to him and, in retrospect, I think I was always looking for Harold's approval. Also, my mother was still a Killins in name, and perhaps the name was a small part of our past. We had lost everything else."

Enduring Mysteries

We have pieced together the events of the preamble before May 2 and the familicide from fragmentary evidence, much of it conflicting. Despite being comfortable that we have rendered these events as accurately as is possible from this perspective, a number of mysteries remain. Among them are the following.

When and how was Patsy murdered?

Why was there no autopsy to determine the cause of her death? We know that Tom picked up the hammer and struck Robert repeatedly on the head, blows that eventually ended Robert's life, to protect Patsy, who was crying next to her mother's body in the kitchen. Strangely, however, this question was not addressed at either inquest, nor by any individuals after the tragedy. No reporter took up the question either. Directed by Margaret to stay in their bedroom, Patsy made her way to the kitchen and was seen there by Tom and Fred. Fred registered that she was there, but he left the house immediately after witnessing Tom and Robert fighting for the guns. Tom would not have left the house had she been clearly in danger, so at some point, she was murdered, and likely by the two-by-six piece of lumber used as a club that Tom had seen

Robert swinging. Her body was found outside; did Robert drag it there, and if so, why? The house was covered in blood from Tom's and Robert's wounds and from Florence's body. At that point, there was nothing to hide. Was Robert's final act in the house one of confusion or contrition for murdering a six-year-old child? An alternative theory is that Patsy was unconscious in the kitchen next to her mother's body. She might have regained consciousness, summoning enough strength to get herself outside, and dying from her injuries where she was found. All of his other victims were adults; Patsy was the only child murdered.

How and when did Gladys die?
We are left with Gladys's and her dog Taffy's bodies, shell casings, shells, and pills scattered on the floor in front of a shattered door. Beyond that, we know nothing. Did the dog jump at Robert in defence of Gladys, scattering around the contents of his ammunition belt? Did Gladys try to negotiate with Robert or scream at him? Were the shotgun blasts delivered from the inside or the outside of the cabin? If he killed Gladys inside, the sounds might not have reached the others. Perhaps the shots from the outside were the only ones heard by others, and interpreted as car backfires. Gladys had a piercing voice, and the cabin was not so far from the main house. Had she screamed, others would likely have heard. Is it possible that Gladys was killed last? Robert did not have his shotgun at the start of his rampage with Gladys, so how did he manage to use that to blast the door in without anyone hearing? Had she heard this, the blast would have warned Florence of the peril she would soon herself experience.

When and why did Robert ingest the poison? And what was his purpose in doing so?
Robert had purchased the rat poison on April 4, explaining that he needed it to get rid of rodents. Thus, he had planned the event at least as far back as early April. Furthermore, he was found to have $3,751, personal papers, some nine millimetre shells, and a plastic container with strychnine and arsenic in it on his person. He was fully armed when he took to

his car. He had legally purchased the two handguns in 1948 and 1952 in Brighton, and the shotgun was even older. This was after Florence had left him. Robert is said to have taken fifteen milligrams of strychnine, which is half the minimum lethal dose.

It would appear, therefore, that Robert hoped he would survive the mayhem and start afresh somewhere else. If this is accurate, why did he take the strychnine, seemingly reducing his chances of surviving and escaping? It is possible that he ingested the poison after the fight with Tom Major or after the gunfire in the Campbells' house. From a medical point of view, Brian (who became a medical doctor) believes that Robert was fully aware of the stimulating effects of taking strychnine, and that he had experimented with it in the past. Recall the manic well-digging episode during which he forced both Margaret and Brian to work at hauling up dirt over many hours, exhausting both children, but apparently with Robert continuing in a frenzy. Was he using strychnine then?

Both of the interactions with Tom Major and with the group in the Campbell house resulted in survivors escaping to tell the world about the murders Robert had committed. Had he been able to carry through with his plan and murder Tom Major at the same time as Florence, and Fred Campbell and Margaret and Brian along with Pearl, he might have hoped that the murders would remain undiscovered until he was safely away. After the debacle at both houses, there were five direct witnesses and all had escaped his clutches. This might have been the impetus for taking poison, knowing that eventually the police would track him down. He tried to drive his way out of the murder scene. Along with his head injury, poison would have made him queasy and sick, although seemingly energetic, that even that plan was futile.

Perhaps the poison was in the plan all along, and he took it early in his rampage. One theory that has been presented to us is that Robert took the poison in order to implicate Florence and Tom. He might have hoped to argue that he was being poisoned by them, and that he needed to carry out the murders in self-defence. After his death, which he must have anticipated after the hammer beating by Tom, a finger would be pointed at Tom Major, the only survivor from the massacre in the main house. This theory also carried the explanation that Robert had an anti-dote in his ammunition belt. If that was true, no one found it and it was absent from the materials examined at the inquest.

Robert was well read. It is possible that he had learned that strychnine was a stimulant, as reported at the inquest. It was often used to enhance athletic performance in the late-nineteenth and early twentieth centuries. If this scenario, or parts of it, were accurate, why did he carry the sum of money in his belt? Surely this was to start him on a new life somewhere else. Perhaps it was "insurance" that he would get lucky and escape.

Alternatively, is it possible that the poison was intended for the family and not for him at all? Perhaps it constituted an alternative plan to rid himself of Tom and to punish Florence. In this event, perhaps he was taking small amounts of poison to "protect" himself from his having laced the water supply with the poison. Folk remedies sometimes suggested that small amounts would protect a person in this way. However, no one else complained of stomach problems, the likely result of placing poison in the water, and neither Margaret nor Brian had any physical problems in the hospital or after moving to Calgary. The role intended for the poison is most unclear.

Did Robert bury money on the land?

There were rumours that Robert had buried money in jars all over the property. In the weeks after the murders, people were seen digging in the land with unknown results. Children playing in the yards outside the Killinses' homes found empty jars that had been buried in trenches and holes. Did anyone find a fortune, or any money at all? Robert would never have had much money, so the speculation about buried treasure stretches credibility.

Why did Robert remove the rack from the roof of his car?

Brian noticed this on the night of the murders. This act must have related somehow to his planned escape, although it is difficult to see how. Did he hope to make the ramshackle car less identifiable? Did he try to make the car more road-worthy with less weight on the roof? Did he hope to make the car less noisy? Or was the removal part of his frenzied activity in the days prior to the murders with no obvious function?

Why were the taxes not paid on land bought by A.D. for Florence and her family?

A.D. had bought property around the province to sustain Florence after he died. To protect it from falling into Robert's hands, he placed it in Florence's parents' names. The stock of property was extensive: in Castleton, in Bannockburn, and elsewhere. This would have been important capital for Florence to begin her life anew, without Robert's threatening presence. It also was the only capital from which the children might have benefitted. Yet the taxes were never paid on any property, and it reverted to the county in all cases. Why were the taxes not paid by Florence's parents, and why did Harold not ensure that the children received this single benefit, assuming he knew there was land in the Frasers' names?

Did Robert burn down the old farmhouse in revenge?

The family believed this to be the case, but there is no evidence either for or against this theory. One of the prime reasons for arson is revenge. Rumours abounded that Robert had collected on the insurance policy. However, since he did not own the house or the land, this seems unlikely. All of the family's possessions burned in the fire.

Fires

Fires played an important part in this sad story. On the surface, it appears that fire was a constant threat and sometimes a strategic choice. Five major fires affected the family within a short period:

- The fire in Ruskin, British Columbia, was the final straw for Florence in leaving Robert for the last time. She took Pearl and fled.
- The fire in the old farmhouse occurred one week before A.D. died in the spring of 1962. With that fire went all the family's

possessions, except for the little they had at the law office in Colborne, where Florence, A.D., and the children were in hiding from Robert. That fire wiped out the last bid for stability for Florence and the children. News of the fire was a severe blow to Florence's fraying optimism that one day they might lead a life without Robert's threatening presence overshadowing her family.

- Fred Campbell's parents' home burned to the ground in the months after the murders because of a lightning strike. Fred was living with his parents at that time and lost all his precious mementoes of his life with Pearl. This must have reminded him of the fires plaguing the Killinses' households.

- The few possessions scavenged from the main house were sent by train to Margaret and Brian. Through an administrative error, the family was never told that this small cache of keepsakes was waiting for them in a warehouse in Calgary. In the fall of 1963, the warehouse burned down, and all those goods were lost.

- A brush fire in 1967 was allowed to burn both Robert's shack and the cabin in which Gladys was murdered. All of the goods, except for Gladys's paintings, were lost.

Fire is often thought of as a purifying element, and there certainly was a great deal to purify in Robert's muddled, malevolent mind. But fire also destroys, and the family's fires were deeply destructive to the stability they needed to carry on. Of greatest significance in the downward slide towards chaos was the fire which burned the family home in 1962. The family had already fled to Colborne to get away from Robert's threats, so they were not endangered. But virtually all of their possessions went up in smoke: clothing, keepsakes, toys, the piano. Nothing was saved. Within short order, A.D. had died and, without any resources, Florence was forced back to the smouldering ruins and Robert's rages. In this case, fire eliminated most of Florence's opportunities to lead a life away from Robert. The loss of her home and poverty kept her under his thumb.

Mass Murders, Femicides, and Familicides

In the almost sixty intervening years since the carnage of May 2, 1963, new terms have entered the lexicon to explain the peculiar anti-female mass murder of that night, now called femicide. Mass murders, too, so rare in 1963 but much more common today, have been researched more thoroughly to help us understand the phenomenon of killing a group of people, especially those in one family. This we now call familicide.

As a concept and term, femicide first came into common usage in English Canada in 1989 with the Montreal Massacre. In French Canada, the term was not used for another thirty years. Understood as the targeting and killing of a woman because of her gender, femicide often occurs within a domestic setting by a current or former male partner.[16] But inasmuch as the Montreal Massacre crystallized the public view about the particular danger faced by women from hostile men, in these two important respects it did not follow the norms of most femicides. The assailant in the Montreal Massacre was not known to any of his victims and it occurred in a classroom. Nevertheless, that germinal event served to make the concept better known across Canada. The most egregious Canadian example of ongoing femicide is against Indigenous women and girls. White women are also frequent targets, however. The Canadian Femicide Observatory for Justice and Accountability estimates that between 1997 and 2015, 1,024 women in Ontario alone died because of femicide. Its report in March 2021 indicated that more Canadian women died in femicides in 2020 than in 2019, possibly because of the strains created by the pandemic.[17]

It is clear that Robert intended to murder all the women in the family (as well as Tom Major). He planned both Florence's and Pearl's murders. In addition, he calculated his sister's death, whether that occurred at the start or the end of his rampage. We suspect that a second child, Patsy, got in the way, and was murdered less through intention than because she was an irritant in the moment. Robert was on the prowl for Florence's third daughter, but Margaret outwitted him and lived. These women were targeted because of his hostility to all women, born from his disappointment at the collapse of his relationship with both his wife and daughter, and possibly other events in his life that we have been unable to document.

He did not expect to have men intervene in trying to defend the women, and when that happened he did his best to kill them, too. But aside from Tom, they were an afterthought: his goal had been to punish the women whom he felt had wronged him. It is doubtful if he intended to kill Brian, one of the surviving children. Brian seems to have gotten in the way of Pearl's murder, and then he became a target, along with Fred Campbell, Peter Miller, and Tom Major.

Robert's crime can also be categorized as a familicide. This is a form of mass murder carried out against one's family. It is closely associated with domestic abuse and intimate-partner homicide. Robert murdered the family because he blamed them for his life of frustration and un-happiness. His isolation from everyone other than his family meant that they bore the full brunt of his violence.

It should be noted that, by 1963, Robert didn't have much of a family left. He lived alone in a shack, while the remaining members of his pre-vious family lived in a house nearby. His wife had found a new partner, had three more children without Robert, and, while fearful, had moved on. His only natural child was Pearl. But she, too, was alienated and by this time married with a child imminently expected.

There have not been a lot of mass murders in this country, against one's family or otherwise. A Wikipedia list estimates that there have been only twenty-three mass murders in Canada since 1689 with the Lachine Massacre and ending with the 2020 attack in Nova Scotia in which twenty-three people were murdered. Considering that the Castleton murders are not on this list, we must treat the list with skepticism. Nevertheless, its point is accurate: mass murders, whether familicide or not, have been relatively rare in Canada.

There are now checklists of the characteristics of those who commit mass murders. The murderer in this instance fits most of the classic features that have been identified. Approximately 94 percent of mass murderers in Canada are male; 62 percent are white and more than 40 percent are over the age of thirty. This perpetrator was fifty-seven and a white male.

Many mass murderers have a "warrior mentality" where guns assume great significance and tyrannical personality features emerge. They externalize blame for their problems. Their motives tend to be retaliatory, based on rejection or failure or both. In the Castleton murders, the murderer had a fascination with guns throughout his adulthood and carried them with him whenever possible. The survivors recall sitting on guns in the back seat of the car that were stashed under a blanket. Robert learned early to blame others for his failings, and then to nurse grievances against these "mischief-makers" for many years afterward. When he lashed out, as he often did, it was in retaliation for some actual or imagined slight. The current term used for this belief system is being a "grievance collector."[18] In letters to his family as a young man, he typically listed his anger at the injustices he had suffered in the previous days. It was an ever-lengthening catalogue.

Physical health changes can often trigger murderous actions. One illustration of a perpetrator's declining physical health is a noticeable change in personal hygiene. Robert had given up on bathing when he began stalking Florence in the late 1940s, and his hygiene became more bizarre by the year. At the same time, his tendency to diabetes became active, but he was so distrustful of doctors that he refused a consistent program of insulin replacement. By the time of the murders, his health was perilously fragile, with his rationality also deteriorating by the week.

Mass murderers tend to be loners, without either supportive friends or family to influence their thinking. The official term for this would be a syndrome of "acute behavioural or social disorder," and this Robert demonstrated. Such people cannot successfully form or maintain friendships or intimate relationships. They are social misfits. Curiously, in their isolation, they fear loss of control over their own future. The only way to re-establish their authority is to resort to force, they believe. Their isolation also tends to magnify their problems. If there is no one to talk them down, the obsessive thinking that accompanies social isolation and mounting emotional difficulties can result in an explosive temper, possibly triggering the mass murder. Robert had been a loner for many years by the time he committed familicide. He had one person who acted as a conciliator, A.D. Hall, his estranged wife's partner. Gladys also tried to talk to Robert, but she became so angry in doing so that her intervention was usually of little help in his later years. Robert's other supporter, Harold, lived thousands of miles distant as Robert became increasingly irrational. When A.D. died in 1962, there was no one to assume his role, leaving Robert's expansive temper and obsessions unchecked.

Someone contemplating a mass murder typically issues threats in advance of the deed and engages in physical aggression. General risk-taking and impulsive behaviours are common. Robert issued many such threats, particularly to his estranged wife. She in turn tried to find support, but no one felt able to protect her because of social norms and the legal structures of the day. He beat his daughter so badly she almost died. Many examples have been provided of the murderer's impulsivity and risks, not only to himself but to his family as well. One anecdote has been provided of this trait: Robert forced the two survivors, then ten and twelve, to help him dig a well throughout the day, evening hours, and into the night, with neither bathroom breaks nor food. The children were poised at the lip of a slippery hole, hauling up earth and dumping it, while Robert dug further in the hope of finding water. This example also demonstrates his obsessive beliefs, in this case, that there was water for a well in that area when it had long become clear that no natural well could safely be dug.

With Robert's death after the familicide, a chapter of the children's lives came to an end. Having lost their father a scant year earlier, followed by their mother, sisters, and aunt, they were uprooted from a life in rural Ontario and transplanted to the major urban centre of Calgary. They would never again have to fear Robert's rages, but they also would never again feel their mother's strength at their backs. Adjusting to this new life was painful, lonely, and frightening. It was also stimulating, opening up new possibilities for the future.

CHAPTER 9

Gathering the Fragments: Addressing Childhood Trauma

———

By the third week in May 1963, Margaret and Brian had joined their uncle and aunt's family in Calgary, and they were preparing to start a different school and find new friends in the neighbourhood. Shell-shocked from the familicide they had endured, they were now orphans, having just lost a loving mother and, within the past year, their father, A.D., as well as two treasured sisters and an aunt. Both their mother and sister had been pregnant. When they arrived in Calgary, both had only a change of clothing. They were without a single personal item from their former lives; they had no keepsakes or even photographs of their mother, father, or sisters.

Their lives were different in almost every way conceivable: from rural Ontario, they had been catapulted into the southern Albertan prairie; from a small country school, they were registered in a large middle school for Margaret and a newly built elementary school for Brian; from their Castleton home with lots of playmates, they found themselves in a more formal cityscape with no children about.

"The complete break with our rural home, school, friends, family — everything really — helped us to adjust, curiously. There was no going back and there was no mixing the old with the new. We were starting over in every respect you can imagine. Thank goodness we had each other," observed Margaret. "We had lived with fear and anxiety for so long about what Robert might do that Calgary represented an anxiety-free zone for us," said Brian. "There is no doubt but that we felt much safer in Calgary." But the greatest change was in the culture of their new home. Would they be equal to facing this future, coping with their deep sadness and loss, while taking advantage of some of the opportunities available?

Collective Memories of the Children's Early Weeks in Calgary

Sharon recalls, "I arrived home from school one day, about two weeks after my parents had left, to find the impatient caregiver gone and my parents with two children in her place. After all her complaining about the caregiver, my grandmother had already forgotten she had ever been there — one of the few advantages of dementia. Both of us were happy to have my parents back and to welcome the two children, whom I vaguely remembered from a visit a few years previously." There was some nervousness, too, of course, with this difficult senior citizen in the house: "I don't think she [Grandma Fry] ever really figured out who we were," said Margaret years later. Still, it must have been vaguely comforting for the children to interact with someone who had almost no short-term memory. Like Grandma, they felt adrift in this household, absent their parents and sisters. But unlike Grandma, they had lots of short-term memory; too much, in fact. Brian recalls his interactions with Grandma Fry: "Ethel's mother suffered dementia and never remembered from one moment to the next. We had to shout loudly to be heard by her because of her deafness, but I could not bring myself to raise my voice. I was never able to communicate with her."

By this point, Grandma Fry had lived with the family for about six years. Her dementia was complicated by paranoia, where she believed people were stealing her money, of which she had little. By the time Margaret and Brian joined the household, she was far less steady on her feet than in the past, so her tendency to wander off was lessened. Nevertheless, the family all remember how stressed Ethel was in coping with her mother's ongoing dementia at the same time that Margaret and Brian needed attention.

In the 1960s, as for time immemorial before that, there were no trauma counsellors, no child psychologists available to regular citizens, not even any social workers, unless the children became deeply maladjusted. Harold and Ethel hoped that they would need none of these rather fearsome professionals. Had the family asked for help, the school system probably could have provided counselling to the newly arrived children. But Harold and Ethel did not ask, and no one offered aid beyond their own resources. "We'll just see how things go," said Ethel firmly.

Harold and Ethel

When the children stepped through the door of their new home, Ethel was fifty-three and Harold almost fifty-four. They had been preparing for years to go overseas with the Canadian University Service Overseas group to help in the developing world. Ethel had been a nurse, and Harold was taking courses to prepare him to teach agriculture. He was an animal nutritionist. Those plans were put on hold for a few years, although they continued to work toward that goal, and about a decade later they served with CUSO in Papua New Guinea.

Quite early on, it was decided that the children would not be formally adopted. They shared a surname, and Harold and Ethel felt that the children needed to retain the identity they had had over their lives. Did Harold and Ethel realize that the children were not Robert's? This is unclear; the family never spoke about it out of deference to the children.

Whenever that topic was raised, even obliquely, Harold changed the sub-ject. It is quite possible that Harold and Ethel either suspected or knew the facts of Margaret and Brian's parentage, but even if they had been certain about this, Sharon is convinced that it would have made no dif-ference to them.

There were times when Harold needed to talk about the events of that day with the children to answer estate questions, but aside from this, he mainly suffered in silence. In so doing, however, he sentenced the children to silence, too. Harold was quite unable to understand how Robert could have committed such heinous crimes; these acts were so at variance to the brother he had loved and admired his whole life that he appeared to be intellectually frozen on the topic. Harold's enduring love and admiration for the perpetrator of this familicide was one of the many mysteries that had first encouraged the research into the deep ori-gins and shorter-term causes of Robert's incomprehensible actions. It was difficult then and now for the family to understand how an intelligent, mild-mannered, and profoundly decent man like Harold could main-tain a staunch love for his brother, who had shown signs of abuse and strangeness for decades and who, in the end, became a mass murderer.

Consistent with Harold's stalwart defence of his brother's integrity, many years later he wrote a long letter to Margaret about Robert, whom he addressed as her father. Harold was then in his late seventies, a suc-cessful professional and social activist. He was a hardworking man who had survived the Great Depression, a church member, a committed and loving husband and father. He knew right from wrong, as he vigilantly pointed to moral lapses in politicians and bureaucrats. But somehow, his good sense and ethics deserted him where Robert was concerned.

In a tip-off to the letter's contents, he provided this salutation: "Dear Peggy. These are a few notes regarding your father and my dear brother, Robert Ivan:" In his careful handwriting and phrasing, he listed every kind, clever, and generous act he could remember that had been carried out by his brother from the time he was a small child until he was in his thirties. He acknowledged the enormous loss Margaret and Brian had suffered from their "father's" cruel actions. And yet he felt the need to recoup his brother's reputation, as if a thousand-page document would have been able to do that! He ended this catalogue of sweetness and goodness by saying, "I once met a man in Welland who said Bob had helped him and got him into his first job. No doubt he helped many people. Peggy, I know that you will agree that he was a good man."

Sharon says,

> I have experienced few greater shocks in my life than reading this hopeful, misguided letter in the summer of 2019. I had not seen it before that time, since it was addressed to Margaret, not to me. The first read left me winded and angry. It was hard to credit this astonishingly wrong-headed missive with its confident conclusion. The man my father was eulogizing had butchered Margaret's family, leaving her and her brother orphans. But once upon a time, Robert had helped someone get his first job. And, based on his catalogue of good works, my father hoped that she would agree with him that Robert was a "good man"? It was enraging and laughable at the same time.

How could Harold have been so blind as to imagine Margaret would agree with him, even at that far remove from the chaos Robert had wrought? *Especially* at that far remove: by the date of the letter he had had ample time to realize the enormously damaging effects of Robert's vicious fury. Did he really think that this account of entertaining projects carried out by ingenious little Robert would make Margaret and Brian feel more warmly toward him? And what did this seemingly callous act illustrate about Harold himself? "The children had avoided speaking about Robert throughout their years with my family," remembers Sharon.

> At the dinner table, when Dad would raise something shrewd or insightful that Robert had done, the children remained stonily silent. Was this letter my father's answer to questions unasked all those years ago about what kind of

person Robert had been in his youth? The fact is the children did not want to hear this information, but my father needed to tell it. It also revealed something disturbing and novel about Robert who, despite the twenty-five years since he had committed a string of murders, still had a magnetic hold on some people, including my Dad. His dark charisma is part of this story, too. On reflection, I finally decided that my father was terribly wrong, both to write that letter and to effectively plead with Margaret and Brian to join him in admiring Robert. I know now that his letter was as much to assuage his own grief and guilt, undimmed after all those years, that he had not been able to stop his brother from murdering defenceless women, as it was to recoup Robert's reputation in the minds of the survivors.

Unable to come to terms with Robert's motives or actions, Harold threw his energy into making a new life for the children in a home where they would be actively supported and loved. The climate in Harold and Ethel's home was warm but exceedingly reserved. Sharon recollects:

As a child, my friends would occasionally observe that no one hugged each other in our family, and I would agree, wondering why people would do that when they knew they were loved already. However, I have only fully understood how unusual my parents were in that regard since hearing and reading the oral histories for this book. One reason for my blindness to their reserve is that I have adopted their ways, as children do. Their — and my — reserve extends to discourse that has been carefully stripped of sentimentality or too much emoting. In no sense does this suggest that my parents were unloving. We all felt their affection, but it was transmitted through acts of kindness rather than words of undying love.

On the other hand, Margaret and Brian had come from a deeply affectionate family, as one can note from the family photographs throughout the first part of this book. In particular, their mother continually demonstrated her love for all of her children. The lack of physical affection in their new home was a deep loss for the children. Adapting to a family culture where no one embraced one another if this could be avoided and where people did not regularly express love for one another was going to be a challenge at the best of times. And this most definitely was not the best of times.

Ethel found the adjustment of having two needy children in her care a greater challenge than did Harold. Of course, he was off daily at his job while Ethel coped with the early inevitable adjustment issues. Thus, it took some time for mutual warmth to develop between the children and Ethel. She was a dramatically different personality from their vivacious and fun-loving mother. Ethel descended from Mennonite/Loyalist stock. She would not have understood the definition of "vivacious," much less have acted by that script, even if she had tried. She was intellectually inclined and would have chosen to spend a lot of her time reading if her responsibilities had permitted. She was also partly deaf, and therefore did not like undue noise or too much physical activity since this could easily obscure narratives that she would have struggled to hear in even ideal circumstances. When speaking to her, one needed to face her directly and speak slowly, especially as she aged. Commotion denied her an understanding of her surroundings. This was a sedate and restrained household into which to drop two active children.

Initially, Ethel was drawn to Brian, with his quiet, watchful nature. She must have sensed a kindred spirit there. Gradually, she and Margaret came to know one another better, and within a short time Ethel recognized Margaret's many outstanding qualities. They forged a firm bond that lasted the rest of her life, and Brian did the same with both Ethel and Harold. In many ways, Brian and Margaret became their adopted children, filling gaps left by their original family's departure into adulthood. That a new form of the family emerged from this tragedy should not, however, suggest that the process was swift or easy.

The family had one huge trump card: "Harold was likely the most optimistic person in Canada," says Sharon. "He expected the best from everyone, particularly his children, and had boundless confidence in every child's abilities. It was not lost on his own children or Margaret and Brian that his personality was at complete variance to that of his brother and sister, Robert and Gladys. We used to joke that Dad snagged all the optimism in his entire family, leaving the dreary pessimism for everyone else."

Harold did have some of the same mannerisms as Robert and Gladys, undoubtedly family behaviours they had learned as children. When he wanted to get someone's attention, he would poke them in the shoulder and say, "I would like to talk now." While endearingly transparent, the prodding bothered everyone, and eventually Ethel insisted that he get

Brian and Margaret in the fall of 1963.

the family's attention by speaking to them rather than nudging them. He seemed surprised that no one particularly liked it. Years later, Sharon saw her oldest brother getting his son's attention by jabbing his shoulder, and she wondered how many more generations would experience that behaviour.

Harold assumed all his children, including Margaret and Brian, were brilliant, honourable people, and he expected them to act accordingly. Sharon recalls, "My memory of the early days of the children's addition to the family, and particularly with Brian, who was more inclined to question authority than was Margaret, is that Dad used the same strategy he had honed in parenting his own children, with an even stronger belief in these children's intelligence and good sense than he seemed to exercise with my brothers and me." Clearly, he admired both of them from the start and was amazed at their stability and creativity.

Blending into a New Family

Brian recalls: "When we arrived at the Calgary house, we met Sharon and Ethel's mother. Sharon was much older than I. I was taken by her kindness, attentiveness, and intelligence. I liked chatting with her, but we had little in common and very little time alone. Margaret and Sharon formed a close bond, but somehow I felt left out." And indeed, his isolation was one of the major problems about which Harold and Ethel had worried, and correctly, it turned out.

Very soon, the effects of the children's trauma surfaced, especially at night. Both children had ongoing problems with sleep: nightmares, insomnia, and anxiety that was crippling when their defences were down. Margaret was taken to a doctor to get help in managing her insomnia. Brian's nightmares were worsened by the fact that Harold was uncannily like his brother physically:

> Initially, I was given a bed in the basement. There were
> strange noises in the house with creaking of the floors,

water heater, and furnace. I would often jolt awake and lay in my bed in a cold sweat, my heart pounding, fearing for my safety from Harold, only because he resembled Robert. One night Ethel heard my sobbing and determined that I should move upstairs. At first, I slept on a mattress in the living room and later I moved into a bedroom. I was now even closer to Harold. I remember hearing sounds in the night (likely expansion of the heating ducts from the central heating) and hiding on the closet floor. I never told anyone.

Brian covered his distress well: Sharon never knew about his sleeping in his closet and suspects that her parents did not either.

Brian was — and is — multi-talented, with different skills to Harold and Ethel's two sons. He excelled in mechanics, electronics and sports, music and photography, among other artistic fields. Wesley, Harold and Ethel's oldest son, was also gifted in mechanics, although in none of the other fields where Brian excelled. That might have explained the bond that Brian felt with Wesley from the beginning. But none of these areas were a natural fit for Harold, and he found it difficult to engage Brian. Rather, Harold loved sociological, political, and scientific debates and tried unsuccessfully to draw quiet Brian into these family discussions.

Meanwhile, Harold's appearance still struck fear into Brian:

Many of Harold's physical similarities to Robert were disturbing to me. There were the obvious family similarities in looks, the lack of physical contact and show of affection, the poking of the shoulder to get attention, and perhaps an inability to understand or take interest in my pursuits and interests. As I had always done, I found ways to entertain myself. I pursued my own interests. I enjoyed the outdoors and sports like football, hockey, skating, track and field, golf, building models, photography, photo developing, aquariums, bike riding, and swimming. But I felt isolated.

With time, things did improve: "Eventually I lost my fear of Harold as I came to know him better. He was calm, caring, introspective, and often self-deprecating. In most ways, a complete opposite to [his siblings] Robert and Gladys. He encouraged me, but I believe he was fascinated and puzzled with me and couldn't understand my completely different interests."

Margaret, too, was afraid of Harold, although her terror receded before Brian's.

> I gradually realized that Harold was nothing like his brother, Robert. I sensed no tendency for violence or stalking or censure from him. Harold and Ethel had a devoted and loving relationship; they were decent and considerate people. Over time, I determined that my brother and I were safe, but I know that it took far longer for him to adapt to this new existence. Brian and I relied on each other to decode our experiences, developing a close and unbreakable bond. Often it simply took the form of a shared look or glance for reassurance that we were still okay in this new household.

Without a doubt, Harold did not understand Brian's differing talent base, but he was certainly impressed by him and all that he could accomplish. From a very early age, Brian had disassembled electronic devices like toasters and clocks, often rebuilding them in better shape than he found them. David, Harold and Ethel's younger son, was particularly impressed by Brian's mechanical sense, recalling how, years later when Brian lived with him and his family for a short while, Brian changed the transmission of a car in their garage. David could not imagine ever being able to do such a thing, and without any formal training. Harold built a dark room in the basement for Brian's photography and applauded the quality of his photographs.

Brian remained interested in music, and Harold and Ethel tried hard to nurture this. Through his music Brian found other musical friends, and soon they had created a band, the immortal Tangerine Tomorrow, originally called the Tangerine Toilet. Brian played bass guitar and sang back-up. But one of his major skills was to serve as the band's road crew in keeping the speakers and other essential electronics functioning. The effect of the band was to extend his musical talent further, cement relationships with other middle-class talented boys, and provide a forum where he could be admired. Many of the members remain close friends to this day.

Margaret remembers the early months in their new home as being less fraught, but as if she were sleepwalking or deep in a hypnotic trance.

> I remember very little about what I was feeling that first year living in Alberta, and, honestly, I don't think I was feeling much of anything. Oddly, I do recall the repetitive nature of certain tasks: cutting hundreds of triangles for Ethel to make a quilt, painting by numbers, eating formally at set meal times, doing simple chores such as dishwashing, staring out the window, and carefully studying the people of this family. Emotionally, this repetition provided a momentary safe haven of distraction from dwelling on the ever-present images of horror that had just taken place in our lives.

In contrast to Brian's sense of isolation, Margaret quickly found a companion in Sharon. She explains:

> I adapted relatively quickly to forming a relationship with Sharon because I was used to having sisters and Sharon slipped easily into that void by being incredibly welcoming and generous. She wholeheartedly shared her clothes, bedroom, time, and space: unusual and unexpected behaviour for a teenage girl of any era! Sharon was outgoing, talkative, involved in numerous social and school activities, and most importantly, she was never afraid to speak honestly about

her thoughts and opinions. She was unlike anyone I had ever met, then and now.

Margaret and Sharon shared a bedroom: the conversation began the first night and has never ended between them. Sharon says,

> I admired and continue to admire enormously both of the children's spunk and resilience, not having faced adversity in my own life. In that private space, and often after the lights were out but while we were still conscious, Margaret and I would discuss that last dreadful year in Castleton, the horrors of the final night, and the confusion of the days afterward. She would describe her hopes for the future and her place in society. I could almost chart her gradual removal from the old life, where her aim had been to become a secretary, find a little apartment somewhere, and start a new life — into a radically different set of hopes for the future.

As she came to realize that she was a very good student who could hold her own with city kids, and as she integrated further into the family and the neighbourhood, her goals changed. Now she thought about attending university and perhaps becoming a teacher, or some other profession after obtaining a degree. As her view of what might be possible in life changed, so did Brian's. He, too, was an excellent student, and so university attendance became a basic assumption for both of them.

During these bedtime discussions, Sharon heard something of the ongoing grief Margaret felt for the loss of her mother and sisters. She rarely spoke about this during the day, but with nightfall, her defences were lower. The loss of her adored siblings, including her special agony around the mystery of how little Patsy had died as well as her mother's ongoing struggle, preoccupied her at those times. Her admiration for her mother's strength and longing for her love came back to her with tremendous force. Sharon says, "I lack words to describe my own pain in hearing her suffering during those conversations. I knew that I had no right to ever feel sorry for myself considering the emotional turmoil Margaret (and Brian) experienced in those early years. I also knew that aside from talking and carrying on as she and Brian so bravely did, day after day, that there was nothing to be done to assuage her pain except to let time pass." And this, too, was obvious to Sharon: the really hard times that she endured were fewer and of lesser agony as time progressed. She could see that this was true for Brian also.

Mother's Day for the first few years was so difficult that Sharon recalls sneaking into her mother's bedroom when she was having her daily rest to give her a card and a rare hug in private so they could ignore it otherwise. Not a woman to take much interest in manufactured demonstrations of sentimentality anyway, this represented a minor sacrifice for Ethel. The family also trod carefully when Pearl's, Patsy's, and Florence's birthdays arrived.

There were few luxuries in this period, but time was one of them. Over that first year, Ethel worked hard to gently acclimatize the children. Both had tasks to help with the household, as did everyone, and they pitched in without complaint. There was some concern about the expectations for Margaret's French, and so she and Sharon worked on that over the summer, using cue cards. Margaret was a quick study, and in the fall, she had no difficulty with the expectations for her in anything, including French. In retrospect, both Margaret and Brian feel that these small tasks and scheduled tutorials helped to pass the time as they gradually emerged out of the fog into which they had been thrown.

In the fall of 1963, there were three events that Brian and Margaret remember clearly that further complicated Brian's ability to get beyond his trauma:

> That first year brought more disturbing tragedy to us with the death of Ethel's mother one night, and, soon after, the death of our grandmother [Pearl Viola]. In November of the first year was the assassination of John F. Kennedy, and the funeral was on TV at school where all of the students assembled. I was unable to watch it. I reverted to bed

wetting, which persisted into my teens. There were many schoolyard scraps with bloody noses and damaged teeth. I was not about to submit to anyone's bullying. I had trouble concentrating in school and spent many hours staring out the windows, longing for gym time or recess. I found no difficulty with the school work itself and managed passing grades despite my inattentiveness.

Margaret remembers these deaths as if they were part of her old and new families: "[Grandma Fry] died a week after Kennedy was assassinated in 1963, and the constant coverage of this event on TV greatly upset her each time she watched, perhaps intensified because of her American family roots. Hers and Kennedy's disparate deaths and my family's murders are forever bizarrely linked in my memory of 1963." Sharon observes, "If anyone had asked me the year when my grandmother died, I could not have provided it without checking. But with Margaret and Brian, this poor old confused woman's death became joined somehow with JFK's and their family's." The clarity of these memories for both of them is striking and is emblematic of post-traumatic stress disorder.

And so, the first couple of years of their new family life ground on with hard times for everyone, especially Brian. But through it all, Harold and Ethel just kept moving forward in the belief that things would improve for the children. In casting her memory back to those difficult first years, Margaret recognized the effort they were making to settle her and Brian:

> I believe that for the first year or two, Harold and Ethel were uneasy and anxious around us. We were essentially strangers to each other. But they clearly worked hard to provide us with entertaining and educational experiences by taking us on many excursions, such as picnics to Banff, camping trips, visits to the Drumheller dinosaur museum, and mini-putt golf at the local amusement park. They did not display physical affection toward us but they remained

careful, reserved, respectful, and consistent in our interactions. We mourned and ached for this lost affection from
our family. Harold and Ethel realistically knew they could
not replace our parents, but what they could provide us with
was a place to grow and a predictable environment. If they
had a motto for those first few years, it would likely have
been "Do no harm."

Sharon clearly recalls her incredulousness when she heard that her
parents, Margaret, and Brian were camping. "My parents were the least
likely campers imaginable, but my father admired the woodsy lifestyle
that went with it. I have always suspected that Margaret and Brian taught
them how to camp, not the reverse."

And then adolescence hit. Before the children reached an easy relationship with Harold and Ethel, there would be the usual contest of
wills, the testing of boundaries, the male sullenness, and female flights of
emotion, differing expectations for school behaviours, and social norms
for dating that were never easy for Ethel and Harold. In short, the children were normal in testing authority; Harold and Ethel stumbled along,
doing their best to parent them with discipline and love.

Brian recalls, "As a teen, I rebelled significantly against both Ethel
and Harold, who tried to maintain some control but received little
cooperation from me. We learned to dislike each other for a while. In
my later teens, as I became more independent and knowledgeable about
interpersonal relationships (having had a few girlfriends that didn't work
out), I began to develop an admiration and understanding of Ethel and
Harold."

The pattern of parenting these adolescents set in early: Brian would
test a boundary with a minor rule-break; Harold and Ethel would discover the shattered rule and ask for an explanation. Brian would provide this,
with some poetic licence added; Harold would shake his head, begin to
laugh, and slap his knee. "How very clever! Did you hear that Ethel? This
boy is brilliant. He is going to change the world! But for now, please do as
you are asked." And Brian would do as he was asked, for that day, anyway.

On one occasion, at fifteen, Brian, a non-driver, took Ethel's car to a track meet at a high school on the other side of the city. That he was able to drive the car there was surprising enough, but this car was a standard shift, much more difficult to drive than an automatic. Brian reports that he drove carefully and had no difficulty in manoeuvring the car. As ever, Harold reminded him that usually one should not drive without a licence, and then complimented him on his obvious skill.

Meanwhile, Margaret was making friends and showing interest in crafts that Ethel valued as well. Sharon recalls their shopping together, hearing about their tea breaks with a shared sweet. Margaret recalls these trips to the mall whenever she suggests, as she often does, that she and Sharon share a dessert. Margaret learned to hook rugs and sew, all with Ethel's interested direction over the summers.

The schools in Calgary were dramatically different from those in Castleton and Colborne. Where the latter, especially Colborne, were small town schools with rather brutal disciplinary systems where both Margaret and Brian were struck by teachers, Calgary's school system was several notches up in size and modernization. Both children were bright, and soon there was talk about academic programs leading to university entrance. In their new home, that became part of the culture of the household and the community.

Within a few months, David returned home from the air force. He had quit school in grade 10 as a rebellious teenager and had joined the military in an attempt to figure out his life. By 1963, he had done that, with the realization that he needed to finish his high school education before seeking post-secondary training. Thus, within months, a household that had comprised four people swelled to seven. The family returned to traditions that David and Sharon remembered from their childhood of sitting at the dining-room table long after dinner was over, debating some topic. Both Margaret and Brian took a long time to become comfortable with these debates since their experience with differences of opinion was that they usually ended in violent pitched battles. Nevertheless, they sat and listened, with Harold urging them to participate, and sometimes they did, if cautiously.

Harold and Ethel Killins, 1976.

Margaret says,

Not overnight but over years, our trust and respect gradually grew for Ethel and Harold. It was not lost on me as I
aged that, in 1963, they had been in their fifties on a modest
income, had already raised two of their children with their
third child, a teenager, still at home, and were full-time
caregivers for a live-in elderly relative with dementia. They
had to fight through their own grief, horror, and shame of
losing relatives to this mass murder in order to tackle the
raising of two traumatized children. I still find it hard to

convince myself that I would have had the courage to make the same commitment, given the same circumstances.

Overcoming Trauma

We have seen some of the effects of trauma on the surviving children: sleep dysfunction, peer aggression, depression, withdrawal, age regression, lack of concentration. We know that traumatic events for children can easily result in all of these behavioural changes and more. In addition to what the children have reported, trauma can also cause children to be irritable and experience difficulties in eating patterns. School performance often suffers. Children can experience hyper-arousal with light and sound sensitivity, have difficulty with peer relationships, and even become suicidal.

There seems no doubt at all that both children, in using today's terminology, would have been diagnosed with post-traumatic stress disorder (PTSD). The range of their distress was broad and carried on intensely for about a year, with reduced problems over the next year as well. Margaret concurs with this assessment:

> In the 1960s, PTSD wasn't a term invented, let alone applied to children. I have no doubt that had we been diagnosed with anything it might have been called shellshock. We mostly kept quiet about our nightmares, anxiety, and flashback memories. Something as simple as being asked to speak loudly so that Grandmother Fry could hear us was so agonizing that we kept quiet around her. Even two or three years later when I was once asked to recount the events of that May 2 night, my hands and body trembled. Would any kind of therapy or treatment have made a difference at the time? This seems rather an unserviceable question given the era and also because any hypothetical attempt to apply current solutions to change past events is a slippery slope of

"what-ifs." I do sound like Grandmother Fraser in saying this, ever the pragmatist!

As a medical doctor, Brian has a different view of their situation:

> Margaret and I arrived in Calgary with understandable and expected symptoms of what we would today refer to as post-traumatic stress disorder. Because this condition was little understood, and indeed not even included in the psychiatric diagnostic criteria for another twenty years, there was no therapeutic intervention available. I believe it was expected that time would intervene and take care of the problems we were encountering. So, little was said or done to help us cope. We were, in retrospect, fortunate to have been para-chuted into a stable home in a stable community and given an opportunity to start our lives anew. As difficult as this was, we were both feeling blessed to be alive.

Some of the children's problems were longer lasting, emerging anew in times of stress. As noted, Brian remains a quiet man, although that is regarded as a relief by a family of chatterboxes. Brian managed to hide most of his distress, unfortunately. When asked how this occurred, he responds, "No one asked us! It seemed as though our past and the tragedy was a taboo subject to be avoided at all costs. We didn't speak of it." Clearly, the family's unspoken decision not to worsen the situation by discussing it was an error, and probably stemmed from that undemonstrative code everyone unconsciously followed.

Experts who treat childhood trauma recommend a stable, loving environment. Children in such circumstances need to know that they are valued, that they have done nothing to create the circumstances that resulted in the trauma, and that there is a bright future ahead of them. Such children need to have their confidence restored in a world that seemed to abandon them. This requires that their efforts to push forward be reinforced and praised. Traumatized children need attention from people they trust. They need to have their emotions of anger, sadness, and loss validated. They feel these emotions legitimately and powerfully. They must be reassured that they have a right to feel as they do. Traumatized children need to re-establish relationships, acknowledging that no one can replace those who are lost, but accepting that new and loving interactions that are pleasurable can emerge in time. To do so, they must allow themselves to feel positive emotions again, of friendship, kinship, and, eventually, love.

It need hardly be acknowledged that all of this is a very tall order. And it takes time to heal sufficiently for a person to be able to hazard the expression of strong emotions and thereby begin the long trek toward health. Aside from a family that deeply wanted the children to recover, what factors helped these children?

Sharon doubts that her parents read any books about trauma, but she does know that they spoke at length with their trusted United Church minister. Whatever their course of action, together they felt their way along this long passage of helping the children move from a position of loss to one with restored trusting relationships. Mainly, they achieved this by being decent, trustworthy people themselves with unusually strong communication skills. The fact that they were undemonstrative in their regard and love for the children was a barrier, eventually overcome when the children came to know them better. Brian observes, "We were fortunate to have been taken in by Harold and Ethel. Despite the initial reluctance and fear, we eventually learned to trust and respect them. They allowed us the opportunity to branch out and pursue our interests and eventually we found our niche." Because of Harold and Ethel's age and lifestyle, they were not distracted by other preoccupations, and were able to devote the time and attention needed by the children. Those long discussions at the dinner table might have helped the children to legitimately express anger about matters, often unconnected to their personal experiences. Expressing anger can have liberating effects, and it might have helped them to practise and extend their emotional range in productive ways.

Positive peer experiences were important for both children, they report. Brain observes, "I chose my friends carefully, and it was these relationships that led me in a direction of self-confidence, success, and fulfillment." Margaret, too, established friendships with decent and creative children, just as she had done in Castleton.

Beyond the comfort of the home into which they had been catapulted, Harold and Ethel's expectations for them, which they easily met, and the swirl of daily activities with which we were all absorbed, the children were supported because they were easy to admire and love. Neither of them presented difficult behaviours that alienated family members; they were positive, worthy children who summoned sympathy from anyone interacting with them. And soon, they didn't even need the sympathy: they were just smart, interesting, good kids, easy to support.

Brian observes that their loving natural family gave them a firm grounding, allowing them to heal. He says,

> Having come so close to death, and indeed at one point believing we were going to die, we were determined to live and make the most out of the life we had been given. The building blocks for our success in this endeavour began with our mother, who showed us great love but also allowed us to become very independent. The numerous traumatic events of our childhood hardened us to some extent but also showed us there was always hope. A.D.'s calmness and caring gave us the reassurance we needed in coping with Robert's behaviour, but also in coping with the aftermath of the greatest tragedy of our lives. Much could have gone wrong for us, but in the end I believe we drew from our roots in making life's decisions, and we had both the good and the bad to learn from.

Of greatest importance in recovering from their trauma was the fact that the children had each other. It is difficult to imagine how they would have managed individually. Brian in particular needed Margaret. He remembers, "It was Margaret's encouragement that gave me the confidence and support that I needed." In their private discussions, they processed

Brian's graduation photograph from medical school, 1979.

the meaning of what they had endured, how they understood this new family into which they had been dropped, and what they might imagine as a future for themselves. Margaret says, "Brian and I always talked about the murders over the years, trying to make sense of what happened to us but you [Sharon] were the only other person that I would trust enough to also discuss this with in the 1960s. When my kids matured enough, they had been added to this circle of trust, all three of them."

So what became of the children? Margaret observes:

We lived with Ethel and Harold for about seven or eight years until we went off to university and they moved overseas to do volunteer work. But they conscientiously kept up communication with us through cards and letters. They were master letter writers, detailing their activities, telling many funny stories, trying to interpret the world around them, and always asking after our own lives and activities. In later years, not only did our own children call Ethel and Harold "Grandma" and "Grandpa," but when we visited, we greeted them with hugs. They were still awkward and shy at displaying physical affection but they reacted to these hugs with humility and chuckles.

Margaret's graduation photograph from university, 1972.

Brian became a medical doctor; Margaret was a college-level instructor and administrator. Both are retired now, with loving families and grandchildren.

As Margaret says, "Nobody has a blueprint for navigating the aftermath of mass murder; the consequences of such atrocities are broad and everlasting. May 1963 will always hold a horrific place in our past, but we have managed to muddle through some healing due in large part to a grandmother who found the courage to let go and a principled couple who stepped up to do the right thing."

Brian asks,

> Does PTSD ever go away? The simple answer is no. The traumatic events of one's life never change. The intense initial response to those events does dull with time, but the way these events alter the course of a person's life is very much dependent on personality, courage, and environment. Margaret and I have chosen happiness and stability over fear and anxiety. We have succeeded in our lives and are grateful to our family and friends who aided and encouraged us along the way. We are grateful to our beloved family that never had the opportunity to see our successes, but their loss has given us the determination to make our lives the best we could achieve. We are grateful to Sharon Cook who undertook this difficult task of trying to piece together and gain an understanding of this great tragedy. I have learned much from the incredible research done for this book, and I am thankful that the story of the lives lost is no longer being silenced. They will always be remembered.

EPILOGUE

Sober Reflection

———

As we look back on this anguished story, we must remain aware of the danger presented by domestic violence in our own age, as was the case for Florence Killins in 1963. We begin this final section with some comments regarding current Canadian data about domestic abuse and an exploration of the risk factors that lead abusers to commit murder. Secondly, we offer some final reflections on this instance of domestic violence that ended in the deaths of three women, one child, and two unborn babies.

The Scourge of Domestic Violence

In our account of this femicide, we follow the definition for domestic violence developed by the United Nations' *Declaration on the Elimination of Violence Against Women*: "Any act of gender-based violence that results in, or is likely to result in, physical, sexual or psychological harm or suffering to women, including threats of such acts, coercion or arbitrary deprivation of liberty, whether occurring in public or in private life."[1]

Florence suffered physical and psychological harm from her estranged husband for years, including ongoing threats to her safety and that of her children. Given this, one often hears the question, "If things were so bad, why didn't she leave?"

To this we respond, "Where would she have gone?" She fled halfway across Canada only to have Robert track her down. Even when she had the support of A.D., she and her family repeatedly fled from one house to another, abandoning clothing, toys, and other prized possessions in a mad scramble to protect her family from Robert's venomous rage. There were no safe houses for abused women and their children in her day. Even today, shelters for such women are frequently full, leaving victims with no alternative and within easy range of their attacker, often an abusive partner.[2] In 2020, it is estimated that Canadian women and children were turned away from shelters almost nineteen thousand times *a month*.[3] The cost of having no safe space is high. It is estimated that, today, a woman is killed by an intimate partner approximately every six days in Canada.[4]

And if this is the experience for urban women, things were and are even grimmer in rural districts and small towns like Castleton, where Florence lived. A recent doctoral thesis by Gail Bailey explores the current experience with domestic violence of rural women like Florence.[5] Bailey argues that most research in this area is urban-based. Rural women face additional problems in comparison to their urban sisters in attempting to leave domestic violence. These factors include geographic isolation, fewer community resources, financial constraints, less social support, and a lack of confidentiality. These factors were all faced by Florence: her house was physically separated from others, reducing any support she might have found; there were no community resources available to her in 1963; she had no money aside from that given to her by her estranged husband; she had little social support, partly because she covered up the abuse and partly because this was regarded as an "in-house" matter; and she had limited confidentiality, had she chosen to speak about her problems. Everyone knew everyone in her little community. The comment from her neighbour to the press that she had not been in Florence's house in the years she had lived there is testament to Florence's limited integration into the community.

In her research, Bailey finds that 63 percent of rural women report health problems as a consequence of the domestic abuse they endure. This is compared with only 13 percent of urban women. Florence was hospitalized from what was then called exhaustion after a long struggle with domestic abuse. She emerged from hospital to a total lack of health supports at the community level. Soon afterward, she was murdered by her husband.

Public opinion has only accepted domestic violence to be a problem very recently. In 1982, when MP Margaret Mitchell tried to encourage a discussion in the House of Commons on the topic by noting that one in ten husbands regularly beat their wives, she was met with jeers, laughter, and shouting. Despite being yelled down, her statement ignited a national debate about domestic violence against women that continues.

In 2003, Ontario (along with several other provinces) created the Domestic Violence Death Review Committee[6] to assess deaths from the coroner's office that had been judged as based on domestic violence. Between the committee's inception and 2018, the committee reviewed 329 cases resulting in 470 deaths. It found that 66 percent of the deaths were homicides, while 34 percent were homicide-suicides. The committee has identified forty-one risk factors of perpetrators of domestic abuse who are likely to murder. Further, it has quantified these factors over the course of all 329 cases. They include a history of domestic violence, current or past (71 percent); actual or pending separation (67 percent); perpetrator depressed (50 percent); obsessive behaviour displayed by perpetrator (46 percent); prior threats/attempts at suicide (44 percent); victim had intuitive sense of fear (43 percent); victim vulnerability (43 percent); perpetrator displayed sexual jealousy (39 percent); prior threats to kill victim (36 percent); excessive alcohol and/or drug use (40 percent); perpetrator unemployed (39 percent); history of violence outside the family (33 percent); escalation of violence (33 percent); prior attempts to isolate victim (29 percent); actual or perceived new partner in victim's life (30 percent); control of most or all of victim's daily activities

(27 percent); perpetrator failed to comply with authority (28 percent); other mental health/psychiatric problems (29 percent); misogynistic attitudes displayed by perpetrator (27 percent); victim and perpetrator living common-law (27 percent); access to or possession of firearms (26 percent). Of these twenty-one risk factors, sixteen were present in Robert's profile and in the circumstances that culminated in the events of May 2, 1963.

The exceptions to the risk factors included the fact that Robert had had no previous convictions, and so he was not known to police. As a previous member of the clergy, moreover, he was assumed to be law-abiding, if somewhat eccentric. Law enforcement officers would have thought carefully before approaching such a man, even if his abuse had been publicly known. He did not drink, nor did he take drugs (beyond ingesting rat poison), but that did not protect against his fantastical thinking. He was still legally married to Florence, albeit living separately. He did not control her every move, but he charted it. Finally, he had not threatened suicide; his threats were to hurt others. And he issued those threats often and with physical violence to reinforce them.

Other than those five missing risk factors, Robert was a textbook case of an abuser likely to murder his partner. He had no intention of taking his own life, but he regularly threatened Florence's life. This terrified her, invading her dreams and causing her to contact relatives and the few friends she had in the area. But given societal norms, no one felt they could intervene. By the time of her death, she had endured this terror for almost twenty-five years.

Florence had recently announced that she would be physically separating herself and her children from Robert by moving the family out of the Castleton area with Tom Major. Robert's obsession with Florence is demonstrated by the fact that he could not accept this separation, even though this would have given him more direct power over Pearl, Robert's most adored person in the world. Robert's obsession with Florence must have been tinged by the sexual jealousy he felt in having lost her companionship as a romantic partner and his imminent loss of proximity to her. Tom Major's entry into Florence's life gave her one final lifeline in her bid for a new future. For Robert, it signalled the end of his campaign to control Florence and the family, and it initiated the start of his murderous rampage.

We do not know that Robert was violent outside his family unit, but he certainly signalled danger to some others, as was expressed by neighbours to the press. It appears that he presented an image of a threat to the community rather than a record of violence. People were edgy around him, and while they observed him with some fascination and trepidation, they mainly stayed out of his way. The storekeeper in Castleton remembered people leaving aisles if they encountered Robert while shopping.

Robert was likely depressed for much of his adult life. The depression sapped his energies while in the ministry and frustrated and angered him. From his earliest days at Queen's when he had been unable to live up to his family's overheated assessment of his intelligence, he seems to have suffered from a depressive disorder. However, this was a period when such problems were generally undiagnosed and certainly not acknowledged amongst those in the clergy. Such societal leaders hid their depression, sometimes taking out their angst on domestic partners, as Robert did with Florence. Robert's depression and his inability to get along with people on even the most superficial basis meant that he was unemployable for the last seventeen years of his life. But even before he formally left the ministry, he took little satisfaction in his work and was isolated and frustrated.

Robert possibly had other psychiatric disorders that, combined with depression, would have made him unstable. We will never know for sure because none of these were ever diagnosed. He presented as a noisy know-it-all, unable to listen to others in any productive way or consider alternatives for his hostilities or strange lifestyle decisions. As for misogyny, there can be no doubt. Comments from family members provide evidence that he had little respect for women from the time he was a young man. How was this posture influenced by his strong-willed mother, whom he seemed to adore? We will never know that, either.

Finally, Robert loved guns of all kinds and used them as trophies. They propped up his warped view of masculinity as no other manly enhancement could. Recall the photograph on page 69, taken with his two brothers-in-law where he wears a Stetson and cowboy gear, sporting a shotgun centrally in the picture. This is the only extant photograph of Robert where he is smiling.

It is obvious, too, that as the years advanced, Robert moved from a depressive state to a violent one. His interactions with Pearl demonstrate this pattern very clearly. When she was an adolescent intent on socializing with her friends, Robert impatiently and repeatedly retrieved her from the offending locations and people and brought her home. Later, he more forcefully moved her back into the main house after she had found a job and an apartment and put distance between herself and her father. When his efforts to control her failed, he beat her up so badly the doctor feared that another such attack would kill her. He was no longer just a possessive parent; he had turned into a maniacal assailant, intent on beating her into submission and, failing that, to death. Ultimately, he wanted to isolate Pearl, and also Florence, although he had less success in limiting Florence's actions because she owned a car and she had a faithful protector in A.D. and later in Tom.

With this battery of causal factors, it is remarkable that Florence survived as long as she did. Robert was a tinderbox waiting to be lit, skulking about in his shack outside Florence's door. Once he was alight, he became consumed with his rage and pain, visiting death on as many people in his range as possible.

By this time of writing, the public policy framework to protect women and children from domestic abuse has been extended. And yet, the murders of defenceless women and children continue. We hope that this case study of a family struggling over many years with a violent man intent on exerting his authority over his estranged wife and her children will help to lay bare the assumptions that allowed this malign influence to prevail. These assumptions in 1963 included undue public respect for a man of the cloth, who was well educated and presumably intelligent; assumptions about Robert's quick mind as a child and youth seem to have placed enormous pressure on him to succeed at any cost; assumptions were made about Florence as an "unfaithful" wife who presumably should have endured the violence and her fears and un-happiness quietly; they were also made about the men who protected Florence as long as they could, that somehow they did not have the right to do this, that his family was Robert's "territory"; and finally, assumptions abounded about the children's rights in this household, including the documented actions of a parent who came close to killing his child as a form of punishment. Many of these assumptions have been challenged in our own age, but too many remain, creating a fractured safety net for anyone under the thumb of a violent man, and especially for women and children.

A Final Reckoning

Were the lives snuffed out in May 1963 permanently erased from our consciousness? Florence's children well remember her sterling qualities as a loving mother, a resilient woman who kept Robert at bay for years, protecting her children from the worst of his furies. It was her example of defending and celebrating her children that allowed both of the survivors to emerge from trauma and eventually build their own strong family units. As children, they did not realize the ongoing struggle Florence had in trying to live a normal, happy life, such was her ability to create normalcy for the children in the midst of her own terror. But in their adulthood, their admiration for her has only grown with time.

Patsy's loss has been difficult for both survivors to face throughout the intervening years and during the process of writing this book. The truth is important, but it has been accompanied by pain. The confusion around her death and the sadness of remembering her agony in her last minutes has been hard to surmount. As a sweet child with the promise of a good life ahead of her, the probable realities of her murder have been especially difficult to process.

Pearl, the staunch protector of her younger siblings, the pretty and intelligent young woman with a spirit that would not be beaten down, the loyal daughter to her beleaguered mother, the happy young wife and imminent mother to her own baby: what can one say? Her loss is enormous to everyone who knew her. But she is also never forgotten.

And finally, Gladys. There is much evidence that she tried to help Florence and the children in their time of need. Without much money or authority with Robert, she lent her presence and a shared history with him to try to dissuade him from his violent path. She paid for this generosity with her life. Her legacy as an artist has not died with her, however. In 2014, an exhibition of women artists' works appeared at RiverBrink Art Museum in Queenston, Niagara-on-the-Lake. The curator included Gladys's watercolour, "Old Dam at Glen Cross." The exhibition noted her work with Carl Schaefer and her show at the Art Gallery of Toronto in 1943.[7]

Legacies assume different forms for each of these women. With varied talents, ages, and goals in their respective lives, each has left behind traces of lives that were snuffed out too soon. Such is the fate of all brutalized women. None of them deserved to die when they did. Florence, Gladys, Pearl, little Patsy, and two unborn children are amongst the legion of female victims of domestic violence whose names rarely make it into the history books, their voices silenced, and their lives cut short. They deserve to have their stories told, to be made visible in Canadian history.

Acknowledgements

———

Margaret and I began to seriously consider tackling this subject when Margaret, a natural archivist, gave me a collection of letters, some of which related to a massacre in Castleton, Ontario, in 1963 that had brought her and her brother into our family. Some of the letters I had never seen, and others were long forgotten. These testimonies caused us to list the people still alive who had been involved. My son, Tim Cook, and his partner, Sarah, observed that one of the limitations of oral history is that the interviewees need to be alive. They emphasized that if we were ever to properly pursue this tragedy, now was the time, before anyone else connected to it died. This was no easy decision as the murders had hung like a shroud over Margaret and Brian for decades, almost six decades, in fact. Were either willing to face the pain of unearthing facts and memories that had been traumatic, and possibly still would be very damaging? The story was never regarded as a secret in our family, but surely there would be surprises in what we found through our research. Not everyone was as enthusiastic as Margaret and I were, but in the end, our entire family offered to help. As the project has moved through the stages of research, writing, and production, from shock to recovery, and from childhood memories to sharpened understanding, our families have had our backs. Thank you.

As authors, Margaret and I seemed well placed to undertake the research for this account. We are biologically related to the two sides of this tragedy: she is one of the two surviving children from the familicide carried out by my uncle. Despite the fact that the murderer was identified as her father, she had no genetic connection to him, as we relate in the book; on the other hand, he was my paternal uncle. I knew Robert only slightly, and mainly through my father's adulation of him. This we knew, but there was a great deal unearthed in the research that neither Margaret nor Brian knew or, in some cases, wanted to know. Their willingness to continue unearthing information that was discomfiting and sometimes horrifying is cause for deep respect of their desire to correct the public record about this tragedy.

There are several people without whose help this book would not have seen publication. Our families have been particularly supportive and forthcoming with their skills. Kelly Carson, Margaret's daughter, rephotographed many of the pictures and produced all of the charts and graphics contained in the book. She also served as our primary tracker: she found almost all of the living witnesses to the murders through her internet sleuthing. This not only added a whole extra layer of information, it also allowed for a series of reunions with people Margaret had not seen in almost sixty years. One of those was Peter Miller, who freely shared his story with us. We are immensely grateful for the information he provided and for his courage on that night in May 1963.

Sarah Cook, Sharon's daughter-in-law and a film archivist at Library Archives Canada, is another skilled researcher. She found a wide variety of official documents that provided important information, a few shocks for the family, and much-needed clarifications. She also suggested valuable secondary literature, posed incisive questions, and organized themes, and she read and critiqued large portions of the manuscript.

Jessie Carson, another of Margaret's daughters, offered thoughtful profiles of her grandmother, Florence Killins. A number of her insights have been incorporated into this manuscript, sharpening our analysis of the tragedy from Florence's point of view.

Both of Sharon's sons, Tim and Graham Cook, read and provided important insights on the manuscript. As an international trade-law lawyer, Graham was able to offer the perspective of the non-specialist. Tim, director of research at the Canadian War Museum and an award-winning military historian, has read every word and many of them repeatedly. He asked important questions and provided sage advice at every step of the manuscript's production. His tutoring in the specific characteristics of literary non-fiction allowed Sharon to develop a new approach to writing after a career in academia.

The late Joan Killins provided essential information to us of the aftermath of the murders; David Killins offered his memories of the aftermath and has been supportive throughout this process. Our thanks to both in addressing this difficult subject with us.

Brian Killins has helped in every way possible in assembling and checking the details of this story. The oral histories offered by Brian allowed us to understand the world of a traumatized boy and how such a child could recover and move beyond immeasurable sadness. He has been instrumental as well in providing copies of Ada Gladys Killins's paintings from his personal photographic collection. None of this has been easy, we know: thank you, Brian.

Onlee MacLeod of Alberta and her brother, D'Arcy Fraser from British Columbia, have helped us to understand the Fraser connection to this story, and particularly of the role played by their father, George, Florence's brother.

A.D. Hall's two granddaughters, Dolly Brown and Anne Martin, have generously given photographs, permissions, and other memorabilia to Margaret.

Beyond our family, Roseanne Quinn has become a valued friend and research associate in connecting us with members of the Castleton community. Roseanne, who grew up in Castleton, is a long-time community volunteer and a local historian. She has poured her energies into this project. We are deeply grateful for her support, for the binders of information she prepared, and for the many individuals with whom she has put us in touch. Several of these people, friends of the family, school mates, and neighbours, have generously documented oral histories of that time long ago, and some have materially changed our understanding of features of this story. Some of the respondents have elected to remain anonymous. Of those who have agreed to have their names appear here, we thank Leonard Bellamy, Beverley Bevan, Dolly Brown, Muriel Campbell, Marla Day, Dolores and Richard Forget, Barry Hawn, Jeanne Hunter, Debra Isaac, Stan Jones, Joan (Ferguson) Kelly, Linda Marshman, Anne Martin, Phyllis Hockney May, Pat Taylor Spencer, Barbara Taylor Whaley. We are especially grateful for a lunch-feast focus group organized by Roseanne that featured Sharon Dodds, Elaine McBride, and Bill Pratt, as well as herself. We learned a great deal at that meeting and through the subsequent discussions. We also thank Fred Campbell and his family for his willingness to tell his story.

Archival support has been critically important in this project. Our thanks are extended to Erin Acland, keeper of the archives, the United Church of Canada, University of Winnipeg, Winnipeg, Manitoba; to Deirdre Bryden, MAS archivist (University Records), Queen's University Archives, Kingston, Ontario; Erin Green, central Ontario conference archivist, the United Church of Canada archives, Toronto, Ontario; Laura Hallman, assistant archivist, the United Church of Canada archives, Toronto, Ontario; Elizabeth Mathew, reference services, the United Church of Canada archives, Toronto, Ontario.

Because of the dearth of documents in this case, newspaper research was critical in establishing the basic storyline. These sources provide conflicting accounts, but without them, the details of who did what and when would have been almost impossible to establish. We are grateful to several archivists and institutions for this information, and to Roseanne Quinn for going in search of these documents. In addition to Roseanne, our gratitude is extended to Katie Kennedy at the Cobourg Public Archives for access to the *Cobourg Sentinel-Star* and the *Warkworth Journal*; to Amanda Hill at the Belleville Public Library Archives for the *Ontario Intelligencer*; to the reference room staff at the Cobourg Public Library for the *Cobourg Sentinel-Star* and the *Colborne Chronicle*, and to the Quinte West Public Library and Archives for the *Trentonian*. We also benefitted from research support from Dr. Tom Nesmith, emeritus professor, University of Manitoba. We thank photographer Jasmin Mori for her help in rephotographing paintings.

To the many people with whom we have discussed this project: good questions! And then, of course, your questions gave rise to more questions. Margaret's son, Kyle, and his wife, Elizabeth, listened, asked questions, and gave calm emotional support and encouragement. It has been fascinating and instructive to witness what parts of this story have caught people's imaginations. We are now well used to having these chance conversations propel us into running for paper and pencil to scribble notes.

Several people have read and commented on the manuscript in its entirety. In addition to Tim Cook's signal support in shaping the manuscript, our cousin Adele Matsalla also served as a skilled reader and editor. Her perceptive questions and keen eyes added to her importance in helping to organize the manuscript. Adele is an expert in many things, including genealogy. We appreciate her help enormously. Marie-Hélène Brunet, a professor in the Faculty of Education, University of Ottawa, has provided very valuable comments and questions. We are enormously grateful to the whole Dundurn staff for their skill, enthusiasm, and support over the course of this project. Our thanks to all.

Despite the sustained and important support we have received from so many, any errors in this book are solely our responsibility.

Notes

_____

Prologue

1   This is what CBC News reported on the morning of May 3, 1963: "The wife, sister and two daughters of a former United Church minister were shot to death early today at their cabin settlement near Castleton, Ontario, about sixty-five miles east of Toronto. Dead of shotgun wounds are Mrs. Florence Killins, aged fifty [sic], her six-year-old daughter, Patricia, another daughter, nineteen-year-old Mrs. Pearl Campbell, and Gladys Killins, age forty [sic] of Parry Sound, Ontario. In addition, three people were injured and two children are in hospital with shock. The former clergyman, fifty-six-year-old Robert Killins is under police guard in hospital at nearby Cobourg where he is in critical condition with a hammer wound to the head. No charges have been laid. Police who investigated the before-dawn [sic] shootings could offer no motive for the volley of shotgun and pistol fire which shattered the stillness at Castleton, a village of eight hundred. Robert Killins is described by hospital officials as a diabetic whose illness was out of control when he reached hospital. He was found in his car four miles from the scene of the shootings and dropped into a coma shortly after police picked him up." CBC News, May 3, 1963. CBC Archives.

2   See, for example, Kristina R. Llewellyn, Alexander Freund, and Nolan Reilly, eds., _The Canadian Oral History Reader_ (Montreal and Kingston: McGill-Queen's University Press, 2015).

Chapter 1

The Great Migration West: The Backstory of Robert's Family, 1900–1920

1   Gerald Friesen, *The Canadian Prairies: A History* (Toronto: University of Toronto Press, 1987), 254.

2   A.W. Rasporich and Henry Klassen, *Frontier Calgary, 1875–1914* (Calgary: University of Calgary, 1975), 15.

3   Rasporich and Klassen, 16.

4   Friesen, *The Canadian Prairies*, 304.

5   See Friesen, 306.

6   Department of the Interior immigration pamphlet, 1907, in Jean Bruce, *The Last Best West* (Toronto: Fitzhenry & Whiteside, 1976), 75.

7   Rasporich and Klassen, 16.

8   Robert John had been issued a quarter section on the fourth meridian of the eighth range (west) on northwest section, 26–49.

9   Bruce, *The Last Best West*, 93.

10 Friesen, *The Canadian Prairies*, 307–8.

11 Friesen, 317.

12 Friesen, 275.

13 Niddrie, "The Edmonton Boom of 1911–12," in *The Best from Alberta History*, ed. Hugh Dempsey (Saskatoon: Western Producer Prairie Books, 1981), 152–59.

14 Rasporich and Klassen, 15.

15 The Champlain Society, *Ontario and the First World War, 1914–1918: A Collection of Documents*, ed. Barbara M. Wilson (Toronto: University of Toronto Press, 1977), xcvi.

Chapter 2

Two Canadian Families: The Killinses and the Frasers, 1920–1931

1   Gibson reports that there were 1600 in 1929. Frederick W. Gibson, *Queen's University: To Serve and Yet Be Free*, vol. 2, *1917–61*. (Kingston and Montreal: McGill-Queen's University Press, 1983), 74.

2   Gibson, 24.

3   Gibson, 71.

4   Gibson, 39.

5   Queen's University Official Transcript for Robert Ivan Killins.

6   A variety of birthdates appear for Ira Fraser in the records; this one appears in the census of 1901.

Chapter 3
Pursuing New Paths: The 1930s

1 Other estimates of the number of members of the United Church vary wildly from this estimate. According to the webpage "Church Union in Canada," "The United Church of Canada began in 1925 with approximately 8,000 congregations, 600,000 members and 3,800 ministers" (individual.utoronto.ca/hayes/Canada/churchunion.htm).

2 The percentage depends on whether resistors or unionists were counting, of course. C.T. McIntire, "Unity Among Many: The Formation of the United Church of Canada, 1899–1930," in *The United Church of Canada: A History*, ed. Don Schweitzer (Waterloo: Wilfrid Laurier University Press, 2012), 8. See also N. Keith Clifford, *The Resistance to Church Union in Canada, 1904–1939* (Vancouver: UBC Press, 1985), 165–84.

3 Schweitzer, *The United Church of Canada*, xi.

4 Schweitzer, xi.

5 Eleanor J. Stebner, "The 1930s," in *The United Church of Canada: A History*, ed. Don Schweitzer (Waterloo: Wilfrid Laurier University Press, 2012), 40.

6 John Webster Grant, *The Church in the Canadian Era* (Burlington: Welch Publishing, 1988), 149.

7 We are grateful to Dr. Alan Bowker for this information.

8 United Church of Canada Archives (hereafter UCC Archives), Clanwilliam United Church, Clanwilliam, Manitoba, Church Board Meetings, Minutes, 1944.

9 UCC Archives, Algoma Presbytery, Fonds 1020, 84.014C Box 1–1, reel #1, 1932.

10 See, for example, Peter Mellen, *The Group of Seven* (Toronto: McClelland and Stewart, 1970).

11 Sharon Anne Cook, Personal Archives, letter from Robert Killins to Robert John Killins, April 6, 1938.

12 Sharon Anne Cook, Personal Archives, letter from Robert Killins to Robert John Killins, April 6, 1938.

13 UCC Archives, Algoma Presbytery, Fonds 1020, 84.014C Box 1–2.

14 Veronica Strong-Boag, "Home Dreams: Women and the Suburban Experiment in Canada, 1945–60," in *Rethinking Canada: The Promise of Women's History*, eds. Veronica Strong-Boag and Anita Clair Fellman (Toronto: Oxford University Press, 1997), 377.

Chapter 4
Reality Strikes: 1940–1956

1 Strong-Boag, "Home Dreams," 380.
2 *Vancouver Sun*, May 3, 1963.
3 "Wet on wet" involves wetting the paper and then applying the paint. That causes the paint to spread out and form smooth edges as one can see in the sky where there are different shades that blend together. "Wet on dry" involves applying paint to dry paper or over previously dried paint and gives sharp edges as in the building in this example.
4 We are grateful to Elaine Killins for this interpretation.
5 Eileen Argyris, *How Firm a Foundation: A History of the Township of Cramahe and the Village of Colborne* (Erin: Boston Mills Press, 2000), 16–23.
6 "The Killins Killings," *Northumberland News*, June 15, 2001, 7.
7 "The Killins Killings," *Northumberland News*.
8 "Berserk Shootings 4 in Family Slain, 3 Others Wounded," *Toronto Daily Star*, May 3, 1963.
9 "The Killins Killings," *Northumberland News*.

Chapter 5
A Perfect Storm: 1956–1963

1 Jane Urquhart, *A Number of Things: Stories of Canada Told Through Fifty Objects* (Toronto: Patrick Crean Editions, 2016), 51.
2 Urquhart, 51.
3 Piya Chattopadhyay, "Out in the Open," CBC Radio, September 6, 2019.
4 Piya Chattopadhyay, "Out in the Open."

Chapter 6
Murder Premeditated

1 *Cobourg Sentinel-Star*, March 21, 1962. We thank Roseanne Quinn for this information.
2 "Berserk Shootings," *Toronto Daily Star*.
3 We thank Elaine McBride for this information. Permission granted.
4 "Shotgun Blasts Slay Four Castleton Man Is Arrested," *Trentonian*, May 3, 1963, 1.
5 We thank Peter Moore for this information. Permission granted.
6 We thank Bill Pratt for this information. Permission granted.

Chapter 7
Aftershock

1 "Berserk Shootings," *Toronto Daily Star*.
2 We are grateful to Marvin Day for this information and permissions.

3 "Berserk Shootings," *Toronto Daily Star.*
4 "Inquest Held in Castleton Shootings," *Colborne Chronicle*, May 9, 1963.
5 "Berserk Shootings," *Toronto Daily Star.*
6 "Four Homes Bereft of Light Etched Against the Night," *Cobourg Sentinel-Star*, May 8, 1963.
7 "Massacre Secret Dies with Ex-Pastor," *Warkworth Journal*, May 7, 1963.
8 Three Women and Child Are Slain," *Ontario Intelligencer*, May 3 1963, 1.
9 "4 Slain, Ex-Pastor Is Put Under Guard," *Chicago Tribune*, May 4, 1963, 112.
10 "Head Blows Killed Minister After Family," *Ottawa Citizen*, June 20, 1963, 24.
11 "Ex-Pastor 5th to Die in Incident," *Regina Leader-Post*, May 6, 1963, 8.
12 "Inquest Held in Castleton Shootings," *Colborne Chronicle.*
13 "Shotgun Blasts Slay Four," *Trentonian*, May 3, 1963, 1.
14 "Berserk Shootings," *Toronto Daily Star.*
15 "Inquest Held in Castleton Shootings," *Colborne Chronicle.*
16 "The Killins Killings," *Northumberland News.*
17 "Shotgun Blasts Slay Four," *Trentonian.*

Chapter 8
Taking Stock After the Familicide
1 "Inquest Held in Castleton Shootings," *Colborne Chronicle.*
2 "Five Persons Killed: Youngsters Tell Sad Story," *Brandon Sun*, May 8, 1963, 21.
3 "Evidence of Poison at Inquest," *Regina Leader-Post*, June 21, 1963, 11.
4 "Shotgun Blasts Slay Four Castleton Man is Arrested," *Trentonian.*
5 CBC, *Canadian Round Up*, May 4, 1963. CBC Archives.
6 Post from Pat Taylor Spencer. Permission obtained to use. Accessed September 20, 2020.
7 Post from Barbara Taylor Whaley. Permission obtained to use. Accessed September 20, 2020.
8 Post from Beverley Bevan. Permission obtained to use. Accessed September 20, 2020.
9 Post from Linda Marshman. Accessed September 20, 2020.
10 Email exchange between the authors and Jeanne Hunter. Permission obtained to use. September 23, 2020.
11 Post from Joan Ferguson. Permission obtained to use. Accessed September 21, 2020.
12 Conversation with Marla Day, October 21, 2020. Permission obtained to use.

13 Post from Maria Day. Accessed September 20, 2020. Permission obtained to use.
14 Post from Debra Isaac. Accessed September 21, 2020. Permission obtained to use.
15 "The Killins Killings," *Northumberland News*.
16 Canadian Femicide Observatory for Justice and Accountability, femicideincanada.ca.
17 *Globe and Mail*, March 17, 2021, A3.
18 This term has been used to understand the mass murder carried out by Gabriel Wortman, a Nova Scotian denturist who slaughtered twenty-two people over a thirteen-hour period. See Greg Mercer, "Red Flags Raised over Nova Scotia Killer Before Deadliest Mass Shooting," *Globe and Mail*, July 6, 2020, A8–A9.

Epilogue
Sober Reflection

1 United Nations, *Declaration on the Elimination of Violence Against Women*, 1993, Article 1, paragraph 1.
2 Tara Carmen, "Stopping Domestic Violence, a CBC News Investigation," *Globe and Mail*, March 5, 2020.
3 Carmen, "Stopping Domestic Violence."
4 Gary Mason, "A National Report on Violence Against Women from 1991 Remains too Relevant," *Globe and Mail*, May 30, 2020, A6.
5 Gail Bailey, *Rural Women's Experiences of Leaving Domestic Abuse*. (Lethbridge: University of Lethbridge, PhD thesis, 2013).
6 Office of the Ontario Chief Coroner's Office, *Domestic Violence Death Review Committee Annual Report*, 2018.
7 Megan Pasche, "Appreciating Female Artists: RiverBrink's Summer Exhibitions," *Today Magazine*, May 27, 2014.

INDEX

About the Authors

Sharon Anne Cook is an historian of Canadian women's and educational history, evangelicalism and temperance, smoking, and peace education. Her books include *Through Sunshine and Shadow: The Woman's Christian Temperance Union, Evangelicalism, and Reform in Ontario, 1874–1930*, McGill-Queen's University Press, 1995; *Framing Our Past: Canadian Women's History in the Twentieth Century*, edited with Lorna R. McLean and Kate O'Rourke, McGill-Queen's University Press, 2001; *Sex, Lies, and Cigarettes: Canadian Women, Smoking, and Visual Culture, 1880–2000*, McGill-Queen's University Press, 2012; and *A History of the Faculty of Education, University of Ottawa, 1875–2015*, Baico Publishing, 2017. In addition, she has published more than forty-five refereed articles and chapters on these and other subjects. A widow, she is grandmother to four beautiful and talented young women and mother to their accomplished fathers. She is also the doting owner of a Westiepoo, Walter. In her spare time, she enjoys walking, swimming, and kayaking. Sharon lives in Ottawa.

Margaret Carson was born in Ontario and lived there until the Castleton tragedy destroyed her family when she was twelve years old. Soon after, she and her younger brother relocated to Alberta to live with Harold and Ethel Killins. Margaret completed a bachelor of education and subsequently taught English, special education, ESL, and technical writing, and supervised professional teaching seminars with practicum components. She found great fulfillment in working with industry to develop, deliver, and coordinate courses such as Safety and Workplace Reading; Aboriginal Employment Partnership Program; Workplace Writing Fundamentals; Effective Reading in Context for the Workplace; and English for Skilled Immigrants. She and her husband, a chemical engineer, raised three children while living in Alberta, New Zealand, and Ontario. After thirty-five years of marriage, Margaret's husband died in 2013. Since widowhood and retirement, Margaret has placed her highest priority on enjoying every minute spent with her children and grandchildren. She is immeasurably grateful to her immediate and extended families for their unwavering support in writing this book. Margaret lives in Mississippi Mills, Ontario.